AF522376

A Bit of History
A Bit of Politics

Harbans Mukhia

A Bit of History A Bit of Politics
Harbans Mukhia

First Published 2020
Reprinted 2021

ISBN 978-93-5002-672-4

Published by
AAKAR BOOKS
28 E Pocket IV, Mayur Vihar Phase I
Delhi 110 091 India
aakarbooks@gmail.com

Laser Typeset at
Arpit Printographers, Delhi

Printed at
Sapra Brothers, Noida.

For Neel

'Tiny' for us

Preface

Ever since the first collection of my newspaper articles and a couple of book reviews was published by Aakar Books in 2009 under the somewhat grandiose title *Issues in Indian History, Politics and Society*, several more quick and brief comments on the current state of history and politics have appeared in newspapers. Since 2009, a good number of electronic journals have emerged thus enlarging the space for sharing one's responses in public domain.

This is the second collection of such responses. By their very nature they are tentative; as situations, especially in the arena of politics change, the tentative nature of one's comments rises to prominence. Luckily, the fabric of history is a little less fragile and thus subject to fluctuations on a slightly lower scale.

Understandably, there is no single running thread through the book except a general critical perspective, the imprint of my discipline; inevitably, some of the critical perspective would extend to this collection as well, even if retrospectively.

I am aware that newspaper articles have a very brief shelf life—week at the most. But Mr K K Saxena of Aakar Books has a enough persuasive skills to break down one's resistance to publishing these in a book form, and in two volumes to boot. So, many thanks Mr Saxena for your persuasion and for an attractively produced set of two volumes.

I dedicate this volume to my only grandchild, a ten-year-old boy who is growing up in an India from which my pre- and post-Independence generation is increasingly feeling alienated; it is my hope that he and his generation will, in their time, find the milieu far more genial and humane.

June, 2020

Contents

Preface 5

I. History

1. Wasn't the World Always Modern? 11
The Hindu, 24.03.2016
2. Kabir in His Time, And Ours 16
The Wire, 14.12.2018
3. As Aurangzeb is Erased, Here are Some Tales From the Flip Side of History 20
The Wire, 04.09.2015
4. The Past Cannot be Righted by Inflicting Wrongs on History 23
The Wire, 31.08.2015
5. Stories of a Rajput Queen 28
The Indian Express, 17.11.2017
6. Lessons for Our Turbulent Times from Kabir and Akbar 32
The Wire, 12.10.2015
7. Between History and Mythology 36
The Hindu, 17.07.2014; Updated: 07.06.2016
8. Indian Historiography Under Threat 40
The Hindu, October 27, 2015; Updated: April 12, 2016
9. The Changing Face of History 46
The Hindu, 19.12.2014; Updated: 05.10.2016
10. "We're Not Pakistan" 50
Hindustan Times, 12.06.2011
11. Atheism is as Much a Right as the Right to Religion 53
Hindustan Times, 08.12.2016
12. After Partition, My Father Couldn't Find His Wife, But He Did Find Hope 57
The Wire, 15.08.2017
13. Babur and the Masjid: First Reference to Ram Temple in Ayodhya Comes as Late as 1822 60
The Indian Express, 03.09.2019

II. Politics

14. The Violence of Certainty 67
The Indian Express, 07.03.2017

15. The Pseudo Alternative 71
The Indian Express, 25.07.2016

16. What's Left? 75
The Indian Express, 21.04.2015

17. Left, Right, AAP 79
The Indian Express, 14.02.2015

18. Fashioning a Vision of the Future 83
The Hindu, 14.01.2014; Updated: 13.05.2016

19. Making it 'for the People' Again 87
The Hindu, 13.10.2012; Updated: 18.10.2016

20. Waking the Higher Education Elephant 90
The Indian Express, 30.06.2009

21. Break the Mould, End the Siege 93
The Indian Express, 24.03.2018

22. Is A New India Rising? 97
The Hindu, 14.01.2020

23. Democracy as We Know it is Inherently Flawed and Needs Fixing 101
The Wire, 20.07.2019

24. It's Time to Let Rahul Gandhi Go 105
The Wire, 19.06.2019

III. Book Reviews

25. Exploring the Divinity and Magnificence of Love in 'Padmavat' 111
The Wire, 31.05.2018

26. A Portrait of Aurangzeb More Complex than Hindutva's Political Project Will Admit 115
The Wire, 04.03.2017

27. Babur—The Remarkable Emperor Who Happened to be a Muslim 119
The Wire, 25.05.2018

28. 'Allahu Akbar' Holds a Mirror to Today's India 122
The Wire, 25.10.2019

29. The Enduring Nature of Compassion 126
The Wire, 24.06.2018

I. History

Wasn't the World Always Modern?

The Hindu, 24.03.2016

It is time to rethink the very category of 'Modern' and its derivatives, Medieval and Ancient; time, in fact, to rethink the whole problematic of historical periodisation.

By most indices, the world we inhabit today is the very epitome of modernity, even as distinct survivals of the distant past are an integral part of our daily life. One wonders how the 19th, 20th and 21st centuries will be characterised in, say, the 22nd or the 23rd century. "Modern"? Very unlikely, for modernity would have acquired a different set of markers and perhaps meaning. And surely not Medieval or Ancient or any variation of these. It's time perhaps to rethink the very category of "Modern" and its derivatives, Medieval and Ancient—time, in other words, to rethink the whole problematic of historical periodisation. Indeed, the discipline of history is abuzz with numerous questions on the theme springing up everywhere within the academia. Not a fragment is left of what was "out there" (in the late C.A. Bayly's words) for everyone to see and absorb with nary a doubt in anyone's mind just a quarter of a century ago; today it lies in a shambles.

Markers of Time

The markers to distinguish the present from the past are understandably present at all times and in all civilisations.

For everyone living, say, in the 10th century BC would be aware that they were living in the present as distinct from the past; some of them did employ the term "modern" to articulate the distinction; others may not have. In Balmiki's Ramayan (on present reckoning, some six to three centuries prior to the Mauryan period) when Ram prepares to go into exile, the more impatient Lakshman argues with him to defy their father's command. Ram then calms him by pointing out that while the present times they lived in (adhyatan) were in some ways different, yet in some other ways were similar to the past and parallel situations had occurred earlier too. In Islam there was the constant lament that times had changed, leaving behind the puritanical age of the Prophet and the first four "pious" Caliphs, even as three of them had fallen to assassins' daggers. To my knowledge, no specific term was used to identify the distinction between the present and the past, even as tarikh to denote the past would necessarily imply its awareness. In Europe, "modern" was first used in the 5th-6th centuries as a descriptive term for the present with no value attached to it.

Division of History

Emphatic transformation in the significance of the "modern" occurred when post-Renaissance and post-Enlightenment Europe invested it with what it assumed was the universal value of rationality. Once this self-image of the age was defined, the "medieval", or the "dark age" of religiosity and superstition was also bestowed an identity, not its own but as rationality's or modernity's "other", thus reinforcing it. "Antiquity", now post-Renaissance investing it with rationality that was compatible with the wide spread phenomenon of slavery, also came along as the legitimising source of modernity. These were clearly derivatives of the "modern". By 1688, the tripartite division of historical time had been formalised by German historian Cellarius, even as its origins lay in Christian theological debates. The rise of Positivism from the 18th century gave a "scientific" edge to rationality. It came to acquire an "objective" existence immune to mutation through human intervention.

We thus get a construction of ideal types of historical temporality with clear-cut attributes, though these had only a provincial provenance, that is Europe. As Europe expanded to the rest of the world with its trade and arms and very soon its governance structures, its displacement of other regional intellectual constructs followed. The varied notions of historical time in the Indian, Chinese, Japanese, the Arab-Islamic and other civilisations gave way to the tripartite division of history which became universalised by the late 19th-early 20th century. For a pretty long time, the entirety of the long "Middle Ages" was set off by historians as the era of encompassing stagnation to highlight the rapidity of transformations brought about by reason, science and technology—that is, by "modernity". As doubts about the notion of stagnation began to crop up, the three-fold division began to get qualified into Late Antiquity, Early Medieval, Late Medieval, Early Modern, etc in Europe for the original temporal slabs were far too large to reveal the underlying restiveness and energy for change. This too has induced revision of large temporal blocks elsewhere. But the basic structure remained—still remains—intact.

Idea of Modernity

However, the global scrutiny chasing it underscores the increasing discomfort with the received idea of modernity and therefore with all its derivatives. A telling example is two observations spread over 30-odd years by the same major intellectual of our times, S.N. Eisenstadt. In 1966, he had confidently stated, "historically, modernisation is the process of change towards those types of social, economic and political systems that have developed in Western Europe and North America from the 17th century to the 19th." By 1998, he was less confident about it and announced, "That there is only one modernity is a fallacy."

It is getting increasingly hard to argue for modernity as a temporally and territorially limited category in origin, as the gift of Europe to humanity during the 18th to 20th centuries with industry, electoral democracy, capitalism, individualism, secularism, etc as its hallmarks. The discipline has come to recognise that this world of ours has evolved as a cumulative effect of a range of contributions by all societies and civilisations in various spheres and varying degrees throughout the past in terms of crops or crafts, trade or transport, culture or philosophy, concepts or aesthetics, you name it.

One specific feature that is attributed to modernity is the fast pace of change. It, however, ignores that the pace of change itself is the cumulative effect of the past. It also ignores that several clusters of innovations at various time periods in different societies accelerated encompassing changes with universal impact. Just two quick examples. The inventions/evolution of advanced compass, gunpowder, and printing in China in the 9th-10th centuries were soon to overwhelm the world quickly, by the standards of those times. The shift of European agriculture from two-field to three-field rotation in the first two centuries after 1000 AD gave it a 100 per cent increase in food availability, which led to rapid, comprehensive transformation of its social, economic, even political landscape with far-reaching consequences beyond its boundaries. The world was rapidly "modernised" in pronounced ways. Stories of this kind are on record in various regions and times. It is also evident in current historiography that besides commodities, techniques, ideas and concepts were travelling around vast stretches of the globe at a much faster pace over the centuries and the millennia than had been given credit, a denial predicated upon the notion of stagnation and the dark ages. Much change inheres in continuity even as much continuity is embedded in change.

Thus, as the perspectives of history are getting redefined, do we still need the old temporal straitjackets, the old labels? It must be emphasised that however "modern" and its derivatives are modified, there is no getting away from the value embedded in these which singularly locates rationality in Europe and to a certain period. What is left to other regions is to assess their proximity to the model in a sort of "me-too-ism" exercise.

How do we then escape the trap? The fact that the tripartite division is a rather recent conceptual construct which is getting constantly modified underlines its transience. In another century or two, it is most likely to be displaced by some other construct, less burdened with a baggage. Perhaps we could anticipate some of that transition by studying history in more value-neutral temporal brackets, like centuries: How societies/economies/cultures changed from, say, 5th to 10th or 14th to 18th centuries? How much more useful it would be to drop "medieval" or "early modern" from it! In the end, these terms have become more like slogans than helpful analytical categories.

Kabir in His Time, And Ours

The Wire, 14.12.2018

Long before Kabir's time (c. 1440-c.1518), with Islam's arrival in India, two religions with contrary concepts of God and forms of prayer stood face to face. If Islam stood for the singularity of God, tauhid, Hinduism was teeming with legends of 330 million gods and goddesses even as the population practicing it would probably be under a hundred million.

Hinduism, in fact, comprised several strands, including monotheism as well as a very strong strand of atheism, unthinkable in Christianity or Islam as doctrines. The forms of worship for Muslims was a single one; these abounded in Hinduism. Islam came in through various doors: through the battlefields, Sufi dargahs and at the hands of traders. If its arrival at the point of the sword clearly created divisive tensions at the social level, the Sufis tended to soften these tensions through an alternate version of their faith.

However, even as interactions and some give-and-take of ideas, especially between the Sufis and the Nathpanthis did occur, the two competing identities of God—Allah and Ishwar—remained intact with this rivalry percolating down to their followers. It was Kabir's genius that sought a resolution of this conflict. If the problem was extremely complex, Kabir's solution was marked by a matching simplicity. He gave tauhid a very simple Indian version.

Tauhid, the Arabic term for the singularity of God or monotheism, the basic premise of Islam, had led to extensive discussions within the Muslim community. No one questioned either the existence or the singularity of God, but discussion followed on whether human beings can be held answerable for their deeds if all they do is pre-ordained for them by God; or whether Time had been created by God or was eternal; even the legitimacy of prophethood was questioned.

Al-Ghazzali, however, with enormous erudition at his command, closed all doors to dissent and firmly placed the faith beyond all manner of discussion. But then, some doors were opened again with Ibn al-Arabi proposing that while God's singularity is given, He can be perceived and approached in multiple forms: *wahdat al-wujud,* the unity in multiplicity formula that we in India are so fond of repeating. In the 12th century a group in Morocco calling itself al-Muwahiddun (believers in *tauhid*) created a movement to purify Islam of its pre- and anti-Islamic elements and led to the establishment of a state which lasted over a century.

However, all these discussions, elaborations and movements were confined within the fold of Islam. Kabir broke out of this fold and took tauhid beyond the boundaries of denominational religions. But first, what are Kabir's bona fides as an interpreter of *tauhid*?

Abu'l Fazl, medieval India's tallest historian and intellectual mentions Kabir as a Muwahidd, says that he had unfolded life's hidden "meaning"—a Sufi trope referring to life's real spiritual meaning above the daily routine—and had given up the worldly rituals. Abu'l Fazl's junior contemporary, Abdul Haqq Muhaddis, an orthodox scholar, tells a delightful story: his father asked his own father whether this renowned Kabir was a Hindu or a Muslim. His father said Kabir was neither a Hindu nor a Muslim but a Muwahidd. The son asked him what is a Muwahidd? The father replied "You are too young to understand; you will when you grow up".

Noticeable is the fact that Kabir was recognised as a Muwahidd both in the liberal Muslim circles in medieval India, of which Abu'l Fazl is the most shining symbol as well as in orthodox circles and both emphasised that Kabir's Muwahidd status went beyond the bounds of Islam and Hinduism. What did Kabir do to earn this distinction?

He questioned two prevailing orthodoxies: the concept of rival Gods and the need for religious rituals for worshipping Him. In place of Allah and Ishwar he conceptualised a single universal God; in place of denominational religions, he conceptualised a universal religiosity. "*Bhai re do jagdis kahan se aaya; kahu kaune bauraya* (Brother, where have two gods come from, who has misled you into believing it?)," he asserted. "*Alla, Ram, Karima, Kesav Hari Hajrat naam dharaya* (Allah, Ram, Karim, Kesav, Hari, Hajrat—they are all the same identity)." His entire collection of poetry is teeming with this single theme. He also ridiculed the rituals of going to temples or masjids to worship God, the rituals that Abu'l Fazl refers to and himself endorses giving these up.

Kabir was thus displacing the age-old dichotomy between denominational religions with a remarkably innovative concept, i.e. dichotomy between universal religiosity and denominational religions. One God for him no longer stood for one community, but for all of humanity. It eliminated rivalry between gods and included them all in a single fold. This was a specifically Indian solution to religious disputes. I believe one consequence of this displacement was that even as medieval Europe was engulfed in intra-religious bloodshed on a massive scale, social peace in medieval India remained intact, though there was widespread inter- and intra-religious violence on the battlefields.

Isn't it significant that over the nearly 550 years of the "Muslim" rule in India (James Mill's term), in the midst of a lot of political violence, communities lived in peace, for the first occurrence of real communal violence is recorded in 1714 in Modi ji's Ahmedabad seven years after Aurangzeb's death. There is no record of any other instance of this nature prior to that. During the 18th-century five such incidents are recorded. Compare this with almost five hundred incidents every year under the aegis the secular Indian state!

The influence and durability of Kabir's conceptual innovation of tauhidis almost astounding. Abu'l Fazl's endorsement of Kabir has already been noted; indeed, the concept of *sulh-i kull* (absolute or universal peace) for which both Abu'l Fazl and Akbar have earned acclaim derives its premise from Kabir. Bulleh Shah speaks Kabir's language when he holds that salvation lies in giving up all rituals and shedding one's religious ego; and the greatest Urdu poet, Ghalib, in a remarkable verse (sh'er) virtually reproduces Kabir whether regarding rituals or the ego of denominational religions to arrive at the true imān or religiosity.

Remember that Gandhi Ji's favourite bhajan was *'Ishwar Allah tero naam'*. After all, the notion that God is one entity with different names and different paths of approaching Him is commonplace in India; this is the singular legacy of Kabir. This is the legacy that the Hindutva camp finds so irksome and are seeking to demolish in the name of Ram.

As Aurangzeb is Erased, Here are Some Tales From the Flip Side of History

The Wire, 04.09.2015

Even as the medieval period of Indian history is remembered by some only for the demolition of Hindu temples and the conversion of Hindus to Islam, we hardly stop to notice some instances to the contrary—when mosques were demolished and replaced by temples and when Muslims were converted to Hinduism, either by way of the medieval version of ghar wapsi or directly. Surely that's something the sangh parivar can feel happy about.

Sher Shah, the Afghan ruler who had snatched the Mughal empire from the hands of Humayun in 1540, vowed to punish the Hindu zamindars who, according to him, had, "after destroying the mosques and places of worship of the Mussalmans converted them into places of idol-worship". Earlier on, in the port city of Cambay in Gujarat, the Parsis "instigated the Hindus to attack the Mussalmans, and the minaret atop (a mosque) was destroyed, the mosque burnt and eighty Mussalmans killed". To the credit of the Hindu ruler, who checked the facts and found them to be true, he had the mosque restored to its old state.

In Akbar's time, the theologian Shaikh Ahmad Sirhindi complained that "the Hindus are demolishing mosques and are building their own places of worship in their stead". Shah Jahan is also on record having seized seven mosques "from their unlawful proprietors" who had "violently seized and appropriated them for their own use in Punjab". Aurangzeb too refers to one of his two Rajput nobles with the highest mansab of 7000 given to any noble—Jaswant Singh of Jodhpur—who had in around 1658-59 "destroyed mosques and built idol-temples in their stead". Yet, the two worked together for the next 20-odd years until the Rajput's death in 1679.

Similarly, there is testimony for reverse conversions from Muslims to Hinduism, unthinkable in a theocratic Islamic state.

Mahmud bin Amir Ali Balkhi, a Central Asian traveler to India in Jahangir's reign was horrified to see a group of 23 Muslims in Banaras who had deserted their religion and turned Hindu, having fallen in love with Hindu women. "For some time", he records, "I held their company and questioned them about their mistaken way. They pointed towards the sky and put their fingers on their foreheads. By this I understood that they attributed it to Providence", Balkhi concludes ruefully.

Zain al-Abidin, pre-Mughal ruler of Kashmir (r. 1420-70) formally permitted Muslim converts to return to their Hindu faith if they so wished. As did Akbar later on, who also decreed that a Hindu converted against his will at any age "could return to the religion of his forefathers". The eminent 15th-16th century saint-poet Chaitanya Mahaprabhu reconverted the Muslim governor of Odisha and converted a group of Pathans, who were not Hindus in the first instance, even as Hinduism is not a proselytising religion. They earned the sobriquet of 'Pathan Vaishnavas'.

The Persian language text of the 17th century, *Dabistan-i Mazahib,* written by a Zoroastrian, Mobed, implies the considerable existence of reconversion at the higher levels and mentions, among others, two high nobles of Shah

Jahan's court—Mirza Salih and Mirza Haidar—who had converted from Hinduism and then returned to their original religion. Neither was punished.

At the mass level, Shah Jahan discovered that in the Bhimbhar region of Kashmir, it was common for Muslim boys to marry Hindu girls, with the boys then converting to Hinduism. He tried to stop it but found that his diktat had no effect. The Sikh Guru, Guru Hargobind, also reconverted a large number and the Dabistan mentions this with some hyperbole: "Not a Muslim was left between the hills of Kiratpur in Punjab and the frontiers of Tibet and Khotan'.

History is never simple, you see.

The Past Cannot be Righted by Inflicting Wrongs on History

The Wire, 31.08.2015

On August 1, a first time MP from Delhi, Maheish Girri, petitioned Prime Minister Narendra Modi to change the name of Aurangzeb Road in Lutyens' Delhi to Dr APJ Abdul Kalam Road. Within weeks, the job is done, notwithstanding official rules against such renaming—the surest sign of decisive leadership we have seen so far!

What was wrong with Aurangzeb Road? Aurangzeb was—in Girri's authoritative historical view—oppressive and cruel and had inflicted so many atrocities that commemorating him would send a wrong message to posterity. Changing the name of the road to honour the memory of the benign Kalam would right a "wrong" of history. Just as was done on December 6, 1992 in Ayodhya, presumably.

As a professional historian of medieval India—having spent nearly six decades unraveling and understanding our complex history—I am unfamiliar with Girri's authority to pronounce judgments on my discipline.

But then, history is everyone's discipline. Everyone is a born historian with equal entitlement to speak with full confidence. Especially if you have learnt the subject at an RSS shakha. So unlike any other discipline like physics or chemistry or even economics and sociology—where one has to devote to a lifetime to master it.

Colonial prism

James Mill was the first great colonial historian who taught us to study Indian history in terms of the religious identity of its rulers in any epoch prior to British rule; hence his division of this land's past into Hindu, Muslim and British periods in his influential work, *The History of British Rule in India*, published in 1817-18.

Mill had contempt for both Hinduism and Islam—a little more for the former—which had apparently kept India in the age of darkness vis-à-vis the march of progress that modern colonial rule had brought. This was indeed the predominant view of India, with some important variations, among front-ranking European thinkers—from Montesquieu to Hegel and Marx during the 18th and 19th centuries.

This image of India's past was substantially modified post-Independence by leading Indian historians who began to look at history in terms of several variables, of which which religious identity was only one. This was a marked departure from the colonialist historiographical legacy. In this departure, the notion of class—and conflicts arising in society on account of it—played a significant role. From the 1980s onwards, even more facets of the past have come to the fore, facets that the category of class had ignored: culture, family, gender, ecology, visions of time and space and habitat, the gender identity of polities, the history of the constructions of the past, history as it was imagined through the ages, and so forth. The world of history writing has changed in the past five or six decades like never before—in India, as elsewhere.

In the midst of this phenomenal metamorphosis, the popular image of history has remained unaltered—the product of a great and organised effort to keep it tied to the singular pole of religion. History at this level is simplicity itself, the kind mouthed by Girri or by TV experts who are otherwise surgeons or dentists by profession. Or by the Hon'ble Prime Minister, who publicly declared that Alexander was defeated in Bihar and that the great Taxila University was located in Bihar, probably as he was unable to distinguish between Taxila and Nalanda.

Changing exigencies

At this level of simplicity, history evolves as something shaped by rulers or great men (rarely women)—a notion not even considered by professional historians any more—and that the religion of the ruler is the single determinant of his political actions, a notion historians discarded decades ago. An equally strong assumption underlying this simplistic understanding is that a ruler's "policies" remain the same from the beginning of his rule to the end, something demonstrated as untenable many times over. Let us take two examples for illustration: Akbar and Aurangzeb.

The popular image of the two rulers is of Akbar being liberal and Aurangzeb being dogmatic in their "religious policy" (itself a very dubious term). That's about all that is known about them. As long ago as the 1960s, two "Marxist", i.e. non-BJP, historians Iqtidar Alam Khan and M Athar Ali, demonstrated that the religious stance of each was guided by—and fluctuated with—the changing demands of political events during their 50-year-long reigns, and that there were "phases" in which each became "liberal" or "orthodox" depending on which crisis they were confronting. This means the religious stance of a ruler was not an independent and unchanging variable but a political resource to be drawn upon as and when required. His personal religious predilections played a role, but were greatly circumscribed by the demands of the situation.

It is thus that Aurangzeb, both as an aspirant to the throne and as Emperor, abandoned any dreams he had of making puritanical Islam the centrepiece of his rule—even as his heart lay in it. In his 1966 book, *Mughal Nobility Under Aurangzeb*, Athar Ali had tabulated the number of nobles from different groups who sided with the "liberal" Dara Shukoh and the "dogmatic" Aurangzeb (and the two other brothers) during the War of Succession in 1658-59. It turns out 24 Hindus were on Dara's side and 21 on Aurangzeb's, including the two highest-ranked Rajputs, Mirza Raja Jai Singh Kachhwaha of Amber and Raja Jaswant Singh Rathore of Jodhpur, who stayed with him till their end. It was Raja Jai Singh who defeated Shivaji and brought him to Aurangzeb's court seeking peace. It was in 1679, 21 years after his accession to the throne, that Aurangzeb reimposed the jaziya tax on Hindus that Akbar had abolished in 1562—and he did this after the death of Jaswant Singh, when tension began with the Rathores.

Aurangzeb demolished some 15-odd temples—including ones at Mathura and Kashi, where he built mosques. Paradoxically, at the same time he also gave land and cash grants to Hindu temples and maths, including at Kashi, and these are all well documented.

What explains the paradox?

The same paradox that led a democratically elected leader in late 20th century India, Rajiv Gandhi, to mobilise religious support as a political resource when he had the gates of the disputed Ayodhya structure opened even as he succumbed to the outrageous demands of the Muslim clergy to upturn the Supreme Court judgment on Shah Bano. Rajiv Gandhi imagined he would be able to please both; in fact, he lost out on both fronts. Just like Aurangzeb, who spent the second half of his reign fighting on numerous fronts, both Hindu and Muslim.

James Mill had taught us to treat the rulers of the "Hindu" and the "Muslim" periods not as rulers whose actions are guided by complex considerations but simply by their religious affiliation. It is this colonial lesson that we propagate today when we view Akbar and Aurangzeb (and everyone else) as merely a "good" Muslim or a "bad" Muslim. Of course, all Hindu rulers are invariably "good", no questions asked. One wonders whether Kalam, the great scientist and even greater human being and nationalist, would have felt honoured to be evaluated through this colonial prism and treated as a "good" Muslim whose claim to a road—that too from some Muslim 'quota'—comes only as a counterpoint to the "bad" Aurangzeb and not as a master of his enormous accomplishments.

Stories of a Rajput Queen

The Indian Express, 17.11.2017

The Mewar royal descendant Vishwajeet Singh's recent differentiation, in a newspaper article, between history and fiction with regard to the film Padmavati, came as a refreshing surprise. I recount here the historical facts and the popular versions of the story.

Sultan Alauddin Khalji had earned a reputation among contemporary and modern historians for several achievements: Successfully thwarting Mongol invasions of India, conquest of large territories, strictly enforcing low prices of commodities in the markets for the common people's daily purchases, declared defiance of the Shariat in matters of governance etc, but not for lustful pursuit of women. So how does he get tied up with Padmavati?

Khalji defeated the Rana of Chittor in 1303 and died in 1316. No one by the name of Padmini or Padmavati existed then—or at any time—in flesh and blood resembling the story. She was born in 1540, 224 years after Khalji's death, in the pages of a book of poetry by Malik Muhammad Jayasi, resident of Jayas in Awadh, a very long way from Chittor. Jayasi was a Sufi poet and followed the poetic format where God is the beloved and man is the lover who overcomes hurdles to unite with the beloved. Khalji embodied the many hurdles. There are just two historical facts relevant to the story: Khalji's attack on Chittor and Rana Ratan Singh's defeat.

But then, besides recorded and verifiable historical facts, there is another set of facts too, culturally constructed and embodied in popular memory, told, retold and retold yet again. Untrained to distinguish historical facts from cultural memory, these acquire the status of history for common people. Jawaharlal Nehru was particularly sensitive to this blurring in people's minds. As memory does not follow the norm of verifiability, it is subject to quick metamorphoses.

The Padmavati story, like many others, has undergone several mutations. Ramya Sreenivasan has traced the wide circulation and mutation of the story from North India and Rajasthan to Bengal from the 16th to the 20th century in her magnificent book, *The Many Lives of a Rajput Queen.* To begin with, in Jayasi's version and its several Urdu and Persian translations between the 16th and 20th centuries, Khalji was courting Padmini with a view to marrying her. In Rajasthan, during the same period, the emphasis changed to the defence of Rajput honour which had come to be invested in Padmini's body. It was in Bengal in the 19th century that Padmini acquired the persona of a heroic queen committing jauhar in order to save her honour against a lusty Muslim invader. Concealed in it was a vicarious patriotic resistance to colonial dominance which also characterised other literary productions in the region such as Bankim Chandra's celebrated *Anand Math.*

It is this memory in Rajasthan that has been turned into a hard, unambiguous historical fact which brooks no disputation. The inversion of a character imagined by a Muslim poet into the defender of Hindu honour can pass quietly unnoticed.

This brings us to the present-day political context. While

communal conflict is not a late entry into the Indian social and political scenario, for it has often been used as a form of electoral mobilisation, what is new is its propagation with the use of state power almost as an inalienable attribute. If the Congress tactically flirted with the communal card at times to corner the minority vote and at others to win the majority support, as Indira Gandhi did in Kashmir in 1983, for the Sangh Parivar this lies at the very heart of its ideology and is now flaunted openly as Hindutva.

The Parivar has long envisioned a consolidated Hindu vote bank. M S Golwalkar had sought to accomplish this by restricting the franchise to the Hindus alone. That is also the target of the present regime, by implicitly disenfranchising the largest minority, the Muslims—to begin with, by making its vote irrelevant to their electoral strategy. Social acceptance of this irrelevance is promoted by a demonisation of Muslims, past and present, in which each individual, and by extension, the community, is projected as cruel, lusty, and above all, an enemy of the Hindus.

It is strategic for it to create the image of the 80 plus per cent Hindu community under siege by the Muslims and to create a long "history" to back it up. If historical facts point to a more mixed picture of interaction, one where Hindus and Muslims do not stand in exclusive, opposing camps, manufacture a dispute, change the text books and let MLAs and ministers have the final word on what constitutes true history. There is the popular memory to be mobilised as its authentic version.

It is notable that no professional historian of the Parivar, if there is one, has come forward to engage in a discussion of what the Parivar claims is the wrong, left-liberal history, whatever it means. No serious book, or even an article, has been written on this theme so far. All we have are loud screams on TV channels and periodic declarations by non-historians that all history has so far been a single distorted version; no one has taken note of the fact that there is not one but innumerable "left-liberal" and other versions of history and that often "left-liberals" have been sharply critical of one another; nor has anyone unearthed any new facts hitherto ignored or proposed a clear new nationalist version of how history should be written.

There is much to be gained by the Sangh Parivar from this strategy. Whether the BJP wins or loses the next election, the social discourse will remain fixated on the Hindu-Muslim question, from Akbar and Aurangzeb to Taj Mahal and Padmavati, and the questions of economy, development, equality, Dalits, caste oppression, cleavages within communities etc will remain on the sidelines—the very colonial strategy of divide and rule.

Lessons for Our Turbulent Times from Kabir and Akbar

The Wire, 12.10.2015

President Pranab Mukherjee has sagaciously reminded us that the soul of India rests in its diversity and plurality and compromising it can only be at India's peril. His advice has the sound support of history. Here we take one episode from the past where similar concerns were addressed in the second half of the 16th century, when Akbar was the Mughal emperor.

Jalaluddin Muhammad Akbar, who ruled most of India for almost half a century between 1556 and 1605 was totally illiterate. But he had the innate inquisitiveness to question virtually everything and only a convincing reason would satisfy him. He questioned the use of several letters for the same sound in the Arabic alphabet, the inhumanity of child marriage, the denial of a daughter's share in her father's property, the treatment of sexuality as mere pious duty rather than a source of pleasure, but above all, he questioned denominational religion as the basis of legitimacy of the state.

Indeed, he firmly held that "truth inhabited every religion; how was it then that the Muslim community, which was relatively young, less than a millennium old, should receive preference at the expense of others?" The notion of any religion-based state would necessarily involve discrimination against other religionists. To seek a resolution between his quest of a common truth and religious discrimination, Akbar established the famous Ibadat Khana (House of Worship) where first the Ulama (Islamic theologians) and soon others—Brahmins, Jesuits, Jains, Zoroastrians—discussed the truth of their respective religions. In the end, Akbar arrived at the concept of sulh-i kul, universal peace, which would be entirely non-discriminatory.

Attributes of a great monarch

It was Akbar's courtier, historian and counsel, Abu'l Fazl, author of *Akbar Nama*, who created the conceptual architecture of *sulh-i kul*. Clearly this was a total alternative to the concept of a religion-based state. Abu'l Fazl elaborates the qualities that mark out a great monarch. Lineage, collection of wealth, and the assembling of a mob are not essential for this rare dignity, in Abu'l Fazl's words; "on coming to the throne, if the king did not establish sulh-i kul for all time and did not regard all groups of humanity and all religious sects with the single eye of favour and benevolence and not be the mother to some and step-mother to others, he will not become worthy of the exalted dignity."

Already in the Islamic world, huge, stimulating debates were taking place on various facets of religion; many Sufi ideologues were enlarging the space that a dogmatic view of Islam had created. Mansur al-Hajjaj challenged it with his immortal assertion *'an al-Haqq'* ('I am the Truth, or I am God') meaning Truth or God resides in each one of us and no one has a monopoly of it. Ibn al-Arabi postulated the notion of the unity of Being (*wahdat al-wujud*), which opened the way to pantheistic or multiple paths of approaching God instead of a hidebound one laid down by the theologians. At times even the authenticity of the Quran as divine revelation was questioned. There were also heated debates on the relation between reason and faith among intellectuals.

Back home in Akbar's court, Faizi the poet, Abu'l Fazl's elder brother, had expressed doubts about Islam's claims to the finality of truth: "Wherefore diversity of practice in Islam? Wherefore allegories in the words of the Quran? If such be the truth of Islam in this world, kufr can have a thousand smiles", he iterates in a poem. Abu'l Fazl was well up to date in these debates. His own intellectual evolution moved through several highways and by-lanes and their influence on him is evident. But one major influence seems to have been overlooked so far: that of Kabir, the great saint-poet of medieval India.

When Islam arrived in India, whether in the sermons of eminent Sufi saints like Muinuddin Chishti and others or at the tip of the sword of rulers or in the boats of Arab traders, it brought a concept of God and a form of worship that was a total alternative to ones prevalent in Hinduism. This would inevitably create avenues of both accommodation as well as tension, as happens in societies at the cusp of change. The society now had to deal with two competing concepts of God.

Bhakti movement

The Bhakti movement in medieval India found an unparalleled solution to this dilemma and Kabir, the saint-poet stood tall among its leaders. He conceived of one universal religiosity in place of competing denominational religions and one universal God in lieu of rival Gods. He asserts with immense power, "My one God is devoid of all attributes; He is neither Hindu nor Muslim; I perform no puja nor namaz; says Kabir, coming close to The One without attributes expels all illusion from one's heart". And "Brother, where have these two Gods come from; who has misled you; Allah, Ram, Karim, Keshav Hari, Hazrat, they are all the names of The One".

It was this notion of one universal religiosity overriding denominational religions and one universal God for all irrespective of their denominational identity that was the Truth Akbar had discovered in the Ibadat Khana and Abu'l Fazl had incorporated in his concept of *sulh-i kul*. This was the essence of his rationality for which he fought hard battles with the ulama at the court—and won. The two top leaders of the ulama, Abdullah Sultanpuri and Shaikh Abdun Nabi, who had wielded great power at one time were sent to hajj—always considered a punishment short of execution. For Abu'l Fazl was fighting the same battle at the court in highly polished Persian as Kabir was doing at the grassroots level in the everyday language of the masses. Abu'l Fazl is fully aware of Kabir and the significance of his teachings and pays him a handsome compliment for it.

The inclusive ethos of Kabir and Abu'l Fazl continued to percolate down the centuries at the folk level e.g. in the poetry of Bulleh Shah and at the classical plane in the poetry of the most celebrated Urdu poet, Mirza Ghalib.

Today, well into the 21st century, as India and indeed much of the world witnesses a surge of militant intolerance towards religious difference, much of it being state-sponsored, it is the Truth of Kabir and the notion of *sulh-i kul* of Akbar and Abu'l Fazl that are a sober reminder that inclusive-ness rather than exclusion, acceptance rather than hostility and violence are far more promising bases of humanity's survival. Intolerance and violence damage us all.

Between History and Mythology

The Hindu, 17.07.2014; Updated: 07.06.2016

The reach of culture in any society is far more pervasive than that of historical facts. Ram's extensive presence in India is because he is a cultural icon, a larger-than-life figure whose stature no real life king could achieve.

The casualty of the creation of the dichotomy between history and mythology is the attempt to understand the nature of both. But they are not dichotomous; they have much in common

The recent observations of the new Indian Council of Historical Research (ICHR) Chairman, Professor Yellapragada Sudershan Rao, that the Ramayana and the Mahabharata are not works of mythology but of historical veracity brings back to the fore the old debate about the nature of history and mythology. The fundamental assumption here is that the two stand in a dichotomous relationship with no common space between them. This dichotomy also places them in a hierarchy, with history being equated with truth and mythology with falsehood.

Evidence and Belief

The dichotomy was created by Positivism, which has unquestioned European provenance. Positivism had, during the eighteenth century and down to much of the twentieth century, sought to recreate the exactitude of the natural sciences in forms of societal knowledge, the social sciences. Auguste Comte, the founder of Sociology, placed this new discipline at the highest level of precision and Mathematics at the lowest, because Mathematics had no objective basis except for a commonly accepted set of values. For Leopold von Ranke, "History tells us as it really happened." It reveals to us the objective truth, with no ambiguity. The veracity of history is proven by the evidence of facts gathered from archives, epigraphs, archaeology, coins, monuments etc., all being objective realities rather than imaginary creations. Certain norms of spatial and temporal location of events form its core.

On the other hand, mythology stood at the other end of objectivity: all of it was the product of imagination, much like fiction, with no objective evidence open to rational, scientific scrutiny, but dependent instead on one's beliefs and faith.

It is in this backdrop that the struggle to place mythological creations on a par with history or objective truth, is best understood, for any concession to the imaginary nature of mythology relegates it to an inferior status. Or so it is assumed.

The chief casualty of the creation of this dichotomy is the attempt to understand the nature of both history and mythology. To begin with, it is a false dichotomy and no hierarchy of status is implied between them. The difference between the two does not amount to dichotomy and they do have much in common. Both history and mythology are creations of human imagination. History, however, is limited to retrieval of verifiable 'facts' and evidence from the past, which is construed as a reality, even as it varies from one school of history to another or even from one historian to another. Mythology has no such limitations. It is not bound by space, chronology, and evidence that is indisputable. Space and time here are entirely created in the mind, just as in a novel, even as it bears semblance of reality. The nature of folklore is similar.

Does it then imply that mythology does not reflect any reality? Mythology, fiction, poetry and paintings relate to a different genre of reality which could, for convenience, be grouped under culture, of which religion is also an important segment, even as the two are not synonymous. In that sense culture and mythology also acquire the characteristics of an objective reality that governs our attitudes and behaviour as social beings. Indeed, the reach of culture in any society is far more pervasive than that of historical facts. If Ram was to be treated as a real historical figure, as a ruler of a small and insignificant kingdom of Ayodhya, compared, for example, to the massive Maurya or Gupta Empire, he would have been relegated to a minor footnote in history books. A good test is to try to recall the name of another ruler of Ayodhya—very unlikely to come to one's mind. Ram's pervasive presence in India is because he is a cultural icon. No real ruler's presence in the life of India's millions, even that of Asoka, comes anywhere near it. Probably a sizeable number of the population have his name as part of their own personal names. Would that pervasive presence have arisen from his being the king of Ayodhya and doing things that kings do all the time? Surely, his larger than life figure as a cultural icon is what gives him that stature that no other real life king could achieve.

Plural Versions

There is also the question of plural versions of mythologies, as there are of history. Paula Richman's book is titled *Many Ramayanas* and the great Professor A.K. Ramanujam was the author of the superb essay, "Three Hundred Ramayanas". The Mahabharata similarly has not one but numerous versions, and Madhavacarya in the thirteenth century speaks of the text teeming with interpretations, interpolations and transpositions. That's a few centuries before the modern day baddies among historians came in to question the singularity of the sacred texts. So, which version is one seeking to authenticate in terms of its historical veracity?

The study of mythology would be greatly enriched as a cultural phenomenon rather than as authentic history that is based on material evidence, without it suffering the ignominy of being false or inferior.

But then, the very assertion that mythological figures are not necessarily historical figures immediately invites political fire from the Sangh Parivar. The Parivar's Hindutva sentiment is hurt precisely because it has accepted the Positivist dichotomy of history and mythology and its ensuing hierarchisation of status. How far has the Parivar really travelled from the celebration of plural versions of truth in ancient Indian intellectual and cultural milieu to the modern day assertion of singularity of Truth, which is what Positivism has bestowed upon us and dominated our thinking for nearly three centuries!

Indian Historiography Under Threat

The Hindu, October 27, 2015; Updated: April 12, 2016

Scholars like V.S. Pathak and Romila Thapar have established that ancient India drew its sense of the past from a vast range of sources, of which religious texts were one.

Since independence Indian historians have revisited all the assumptions of colonial historiography; religious identities were no more the determining element. History was no longer mono-causal but multifaceted to include social and economic structures.

The old colonial notion that ancient Indians had no sense of history has by now been blown to bits by outstanding scholars like V. S. Pathak and Romila Thapar. They have also established that ancient India drew its sense of the past from a vast range of sources, of which religious texts were one, and that its understanding of the past differed radically from the Western notions of history. Romila Thapar, in particular in her magisterial work, *The Past Before Us—Historical Traditions of Early North India* (published 2013), scrutinises the vast corpus of Vedic texts, the great epics Ramayana and Mahabharata, the itihas-purana traditions, the Buddhist and Jain canonical texts, hagiographies, biographies, inscriptions, chronicles and theatrical compositions like the Mudrarakshasa to form her database and arrives at conclusions which frontally challenge received wisdom from the West.

Court Narratives

Come medieval India and a new genre of history comes alive. These histories, more like court chronicles, titled Tawarikh, plural of tarikh which denotes both date and history, followed strict codes of chronological and spatial location of an event and were narrative rather than analytical in content, although a certain view point always inheres in any narrative account . There was an interesting dichotomy as part of the narrative. The framework that enclosed the tawarikh was largely derived from Islam, which not only brought a new religion to the world but also a new concept of history. The chronological framework that was almost invariably followed was that of the Islamic hijri era, with the exception of Abul Fazl, Akbar's courtier and historian. Abul Fazl abandoned it in favour of Ilahi era, created to commemorate Akbar's accession to the throne, and disengaged history writing from the axis of Islam. At any rate, Abul Fazl had rather a low opinion of the hijri era. Within this overall chronological framework, historians were more particular about locating each event in the precise year of the reign of each ruler whose deeds formed their main narrative.

More important, they did not look at history as a branch of Islamic theology, unlike their European counterparts. In medieval Europe, histories composed by church fathers, the only literate class, perceived all historical events as manifestations of God's will. For them the past, present and future—all constituted part of God's grand design in which nothing happened haphazardly, even as these appeared so to human beings. In medieval India, on the other hand, historical events are treated as individual, independent events and not part of a grand pattern, and historical causation is established in human volition and at best human nature. God is invoked only when the historian is unsure of the veracity of an event, akin to our everyday invocation, "God knows" when we are unsure of something.

We are thus introduced to "strong" or "weak" rulers, "liberal" or "orthodox" rulers and the complete history of their reigns merely unfolds their nature. Best examples: Muhammad bin Tughlaq ("his nature consisting of contradictory qualities"), Akbar ("liberal"), Aurangzeb ("orthodox"). Diversity necessarily inhered in the explanation since no two persons, not even rulers, would possess the same nature.

Colonial Invention

It was James Mill who metamorphosed the entire, long history of ancient and medieval India, divesting it of all its diversities by making the religious identity of the rulers, instead of their nature, the central category for understanding the past; all diversity of explanation was lost to the uniformity of the religious identity of all the rulers, whether Hindu or Muslim. His *History of British Rule*, published in 1818, created the tripartite division of India's past into the Hindu, the Muslim and the British periods. As a Utilitarian and as a colonialist par excellence, he had contempt for religion, for both Hinduism and Islam but more for the former, and emphasised that prior to the British rule, India was mired in religious obscurantism with no worthwhile achievement to its credit; thus the Indians ought to be thankful to the colonialists for setting them on the path of progress.

This was further reinforced by Elliot and Dowson's 8-volume *History of India as told by its own Historians,* published from 1854 onward, bluntly stating in the

Introduction: "This history will teach the bombastic babus of India the great benefits British rule has brought them." The foundation of the infamous "divide and rule" strategy had been laid.

Since then the tripartite division has remained operative in the teaching of history in India and even when the nomenclature was altered to Ancient, Medieval and Modern, first by Stanley Lane-Poole in 1903, the basis of division remained the same until around the early 1960s. Religious identity and religious conflict were clearly the central analytical categories in this history. Fundamental to it was the assumption that colonialism was the harbinger of "modernity" to India, as it was to the rest of Asia, Africa and Latin America. This view was shared by almost all European thinkers during the 18th and 19th centuries from Montesquieu to Karl Marx, even as their modes of thought as well as their sympathies were as different from one another as chalk was from cheese.

From the late 1950s and 60s, Indian historians began to revisit all the assumptions and categories of historiography handed down to them by colonialism. A few, indeed very few, of the historians who fundamentally revised colonial history writing were committed Marxists and many more were not. It is the Marxists who questioned even Marx's understanding of India's past, including his notion of the Asiatic Mode of Production. One substitute for it was the concept of "Indian Feudalism", but this was soon thrown open, with the question "Was There Feudalism in Indian History?"—the title of an essay that became the centre of a long-drawn, international debate, which unearthed several facets that lay unseen below the surface. The long cherished colonial notion that India (indeed the Orient) was unfamiliar with any socio-economic mutations before the colonial engine of modernity was set in motion, was blown to smithereens.

Religious identities were assigned their due priority in the saga of change, but were no more the lone, determining element. History was no longer mono-causal but multifaceted. Sights were moved from individual character of rulers to social and economic structures, technology and trade as the motors of change, uprisings of peasants and artisans against the state's exploitative excesses. A threshold had been crossed.

From the 1980s and 90s yet another threshold was crossed when still newer problematics, themes, newer methods of looking at history evolved. The history of women and gender, ecology, inter-personal relations, sexuality, history of the notions of time, space, habitats, of perceptions of masculinity and femininity, the nature of polities, alternative views of history evident in the vernacular languages, the enormous dynamism of Hindu philosophy especially in the 17th century, the evolution of Bhakti culture and worldview in opposition to elite Brahamanic culture, the formation of identities and most important the recognition of and respect for immense diversity in the perceptions of the past either as a mega narrative or as individual events such as the Partition of India—all these and more have taken us a long, very long, distance from the colonialist and even Marxist historiography. We live in a fascinatingly fast-moving environment.

Hindutva Discomfort

It is this immense diversity and its inescapable premise—discussion, disputation and debate at a level of professional competence—that the Hindutva brigade finds so uncomfortable, largely because history can no longer revert to mono-causal explanations, which is its sole and entire worldview. It is no surprise that while we had some outstanding professional historians down to the 1960s, like R.C. Majumdar, who were committed to the "Hindu" version of history and were yet deeply rooted in the discipline, the Hindutva brigade has since failed to produce any notable professional historian. The new developments in the discipline have passed them by.

The categories created by colonialism have been abandoned even by the British scholars as a consequence of interaction with Indian historians. But the present regime, guided and controlled by the RSS, is still sticking to them with unprecedented fervour. Ironically, the Hindutva brigade touts its claim to "Indianising" Indian history as a giant step towards cleansing it of colonialist (and Marxist) pollutants. How masterfully George Orwell had in his fictional Nineteen Eighty Four portrayed the crucial role of "doublespeak" in running a duplicitous state system.

The Changing Face of History

The Hindu, 19.12.2014; Updated: 05.10.2016

The Positivist postulate of mythology as implicitly fictitious is the reason for the anxiety in projecting mythological stories as historical events.

Whenever the State has intervened to determine what history should be taught to its citizens, the result has been an unmitigated disaster both for the discipline and for the society.

Over the past five odd decades the face of History as a discipline has undergone amazing transformations. During the 18th, 19th and much of the 20th century, History, much like other science and social science disciplines, was dominated by the Positivist or Marxist paradigm which had posited an objective reality out there amenable to recovery through incremental knowledge of facts which would ultimately reveal the truth. Ranke's famous dictum captures this paradigm pithily: History tells us as it really happened. The embedded certitude of the existence of a singular, unambiguous Truth and its recovery was premised here, emulating the methods of natural sciences. 'Scientific History' was the elevating phrase used by its practitioners. It also had a clearly European provenance.

Over the decades the realisation grew that unlike the facts of the natural sciences which are given and immutable, social 'facts' resulting from human action are malleable.

History as a social science does not have the luxury of a single Truth, but diverse truths, open to a variety of interpretations. The Positivist/Marxist certitude began to give way to ambiguities in the last quarter of the twentieth century, which in turn opened up elusive areas of study, beyond the hard facts of battles, coronations, depositions and trade figures. Evolving codes of human behaviour imbibed through daily lived experience, moral dimensions inherent in religions, mythologies and cultures, changing images of the past, including origin myths, and changing perceptions of time and space, and much more called out to the historian for attention. All of these led to not one but several directions.

Questioning Eurocentric History

One direction that opened up was questioning the Eurocentric history of the world. For ages the assumption that the West was the driver of the universe we inhabit was a given, that the 'modern' world was what the West had made it and it got reflected in the view of the past globally. That 'Globalisation' and 'Modernity' were given to humanity by the West was taken for granted. Today, in the past few decades, both have been severely problematised and both are sometimes getting traced as far as we can go back in history around the world. In lieu of a Eurocentric history, the consensus among professional historians all around is that the world we inhabit was made up of contributions from all societies, civilisations and cultures throughout the past, whether in the arena of crops, techniques, astronomy, mathematics, philosophy, ideas, cultural mores, whatever.

This is as much the result of an opening up of the notion of diversities as its reinforcement. Positivism, by emphasising the singularity of Truth, had differentiated between history as the embodiment of the Truth and mythology as its opposite, implicitly fictitious. The use of 'myth' for mythology was especially conducive to this misunderstanding. The evolving vision, however, looks at mythology too as comprising 'facts', although of a different order than the facts of historical events. Mythology actually has a much wider reach in all human societies than historical facts have and requires a much subtler comprehension. Thus, the study of mythologies of different societies and cultures brings to the surface a whole range of values they had imbibed over the millennia underneath the overarching good vs. evil syndrome. So too with the study of the arts—theatre, poetry, paintings... The Positivist postulate of mythology as implicitly fictitious is the reason for the anxiety in projecting mythological stories as historical events, leading to absurd claims like the existence of nuclear bombs, stem cell research and head transplantation in ancient India. One wonders why Indian rulers, in possession of nuclear weapons, incessantly kept losing one battle after another to a host of invaders throughout history since several centuries BC!

Other Diversities

Two other diversities came to the fore. For long, history had a mono-causal explanation: conflict between civilisations embodied in religious difference. The Christian crusades against Muslims, the 'Muslim' rule in medieval India and so forth. All other facets that contribute to social and historical change were subsumed in it. Today, religion is one among a milieu of facets which constitute historical causation and historical change, important but not determinist. Indeed, no single facet is given the determinist status.

Second, the great diversity of perceptions of the past, or

history, in different civilisations, hitherto concealed under the layer of the Western conception of history, is getting increasingly articulated with ever growing confidence. Jack Goody in his book *The Theft of History* (2006) has detailed how the many diverse notions of time, space and history around the world were almost whisked away to create space for the Western notion of the 'Idea of Progress in History'. The very distinctive perceptions of the past in ancient India have been most definitively brought to light by Romila Thapar in her magnificent and massive recent work, *The Past before Us: Historical Traditions in Early North India* (2013). The exercise is an ongoing one globally.

In the midst of the enormity of change in the discipline of History, one lesson remains constant: whenever and wherever the State has intervened to determine what history should be taught to its citizens, the result has invariably been an unmitigated disaster both for the discipline and for the society. The most recent examples of it are the Soviet Union and the Pakistani State's interventions. History's evolution through its own momentum has brought unprecedented dynamism to it; State's immediate needs to legitimise itself and its actions through a forcible rewriting of history have invariably stunted both or taken them back. Is this the path the Ministry of Human Resource Development has decided to tread? It is best to hope otherwise.

"We're Not Pakistan"

Hindustan Times, 12.06.2011

Samar Halarnkar's concern in his article, Terror has a religion ('Maha Bharat', January 13), that India may have to encounter radicalisation of two religious communities—even as Pakistan is threatened by the radicalisation of just one—is understandable. But the issues go well beyond his parameters. I focus on two of them: the divergent nature of religions and of histories of even the same religion.

The nature of the Hindu religion, itself a doubtful term, is very different from Christianity and Islam. It doesn't profess a truth revealed through a prophet in a specific book; nor does it have the notion of the Judgement Day. The absence of one single truth creates space for plurality of modes of faith in god and afterlife, including the denial of god's existence. Hinduism then can't be a religion of proselytisation. Tolerance of divergent views is integral to it. The Sangh parivar's repeated attempts to alter the nature of Hinduism shows its poor understanding.

Christianity and Islam are claimants to the monopoly of revealed 'ultimate truth', which defines every other faith as false and must be vanquished. The exclusive possession of the truth legitimises conversion of others and the belief in its final universal triumph. This has propelled propagation of these religions through persuasion but also through violence. It's also the propeller of jihad today.

However, between the claim to monopoly of truth and the historical evolution of humankind, much has changed. Even proselytising religions have accepted the existential reality of the diversity of faiths. If they haven't given up the notional claim to monopoly of the truth, the empirical acceptance of diversity does dilute their belief—and the struggle—for the final universal triumph. Their own histories have been marked by diversities and 'deviations' from their versions of the truth.

It's hard to speak of Christianity and Islam in the singular. Besides the various sects in Christianity, the history of the Church itself has been of constant adjustments with changing reality. For example, early Christianity had the notion of heaven and hell for the pious and the impious. But lots of Christians fell in-between the two categories. The Church woke up to the reality and from sometime around the second millennium, the notion of Purgatory began to evolve where the intermediate souls could purge themselves of sins before the Day of Judgement.

Islam also has had numerous sects and diverse views, often going beyond moderate differences. Even as Prophet Muhammad's body waited to be buried, differences over whether a khalifa or an imam should succeed him sowed the seeds of the two major sects: the Sunnis and the Shias. There were other powerful divergent voices. The Sufi, Ibn al-Arabi's enunciation of the doctrine of 'wahdat al-wujud' (unity of being) implied the unity of all religious experiences. Mansur's exclamation, 'an al-haq' (I am the Truth, or the Truth, i.e. God rests in every individual being) was perceived as fundamentally challenging the legitimacy of Islam as the ultimate revealed truth. He had to pay for it with his life. The conflict between the Sufis' and the ulema's versions of Islam are part of folklore. The differences between regional variants of the Muslim community are far too apparent to be ignored.

Through their histories, the zeal of proselytising religions has greatly subsided. While media often goes into legitimising hype over the explosive actions of militants, the silent consequences of massive conversion drives fail to draw attention. If the ghastly recent events in Pakistan have alarmed us into fearing a similar turn of events twice over in India, it's imperative to remember that despite grave provocations by exploding bombs in temples, dargahs and mosques, there have been no noticeable riots since 1992-93, except the state-sponsored Gujarat 'riots' of 2002.

We also need to remember that over a year ago, 6,000 Muslim theologians had gathered in Hyderabad with the single agenda of denouncing terrorism. Are we then to feel complacent in our environment? Far from it. But our worries need to be placed in a perspective. A multi-religious society has a different set of dynamics from a largely mono-religious one.

Atheism is as Much a Right as the Right to Religion

Hindustan Times, 08.12.2016

Disbelief in god has been a trait of most civilisations. But then, the denial of the freedom to disbelieve is being premised on the assertion of one truth as the single Truth, which is backed by the power of political dispensation that ironically seeks legitimacy in upholding ancient values

In major philosophical systems, there was incessant argument whether the world had an eternal existence or had been created at one time or another.

The recent event in Mathura, where an old swami-turned-atheist, Balendu Swami, wished to organise a private conclave for discussion of his (un)belief was manhandled because he had hurt the religious sentiments of the believers, both Hindu and Muslim, is, apart from being a violation of one's constitutional rights, also brings to the fore the very long history and persistence of atheism in human civilisation. Chinese civilisation has done without god for much of its durable life, although it has evolved the notion of Heaven. Indeed, the Catholic missionaries who arrived in China from Europe had to translate god as the Lord of Heaven. Several Greek philosophers from the sixth century BCE were self-proclaimed atheists. In the world of Islam, if the existence of god was not denied, some prominent philosophers like al-Razi questioned the legitimacy of prophethood in general, including that of Muhammad and even the divinity of the Quranic verses. In the Hindu realm, only the Vedanta, especially the later version of Nyaya-Vaisesika, were theistic; by contrast Buddhism, Jainism, Purva-Mimansa, Samkhya, Lokayata and the original Nyaya-Vaisesika were philosophies of committed atheism, to cite from late Debiprasad Chattopadhyaya's book *Indian Atheism*.

In major philosophical systems, there was incessant argument whether the world had an eternal existence or had been created at one time or another. In the first case, nature had so evolved through its own internal dynamism as to form the planets, the earth, the stars, the universe with no intervention from an extraneous source. In the second, a Creator was envisaged who created the universe of his (sic!) own will and gave it a functional, regulatory order. The need for a Creator stands on the weakest ground, for if the universe could not come into existence without the helping hand of a Creator, then logically the Creator would also have been created. The materialists in the Hindu pantheon of philosophy like the Charvakas argued that it is the interaction of various matters which resulted in the creation of a phenomenon which is different from all its individual constituents. The examples they gave were two, among several: no individual ingredient of *pan* (betel) is capable of yielding the red colour on one's lips; the colour emerges from the mixture of all elements of the *pan*. Similarly, no ingredient of liquor can produce intoxication by itself; it is the process of mixture of all the elements that creates the effect. The universe was similarly formed as various gases interacted and consolidated over hundreds of millennia and it became self-regulating. Did we hear the early echoes of the Big Bang here?

Even as the issues were widely disputed and discussed among theists and atheists and within each group, a major social transformation had occurred around two millennia ago. While the ancient societies everywhere were marked by multiplicity of beliefs as well as unbeliefs, hosting polytheistic, pantheistic, animist, anthropomorphic, naturalist forms of deities and beliefs as well as denial of beliefs, thus creating a wide spectrum with ample space for all, the assertion of a single truth in the monotheistic representation of god completely changed the scenario. The intervention of a monotheistic god with Christianity altered the very terms of debate as it were. Judaism too is monotheistic, for sure, but unlike Christianity, it is not a proselytising religion even as voluntary conversion to it by individuals under some strict conditions is permissible. As a proselytising religion, Christianity laid claims to monopoly of the singularity of truth revealed to humanity through Jesus, son of god. Implicit in it was also the falsity of all other faiths, an inevitable and irreconcilable conflict with them and its own ultimate universal triumph. This premise was later inherited by Islam with the same characteristics. Interestingly, these are also integral to the inveterate adversary of all religions, i.e. Marxism. Conflict with others and victory over them is inescapable in the claims over the monopoly of the single truth. It is thus that the whole of humanity must turn Christian, Muslim or socialist, depending on one's partiality. A major agency in the enforcement of the singularity of truth has been State power. However, history has led humanity even within the respective spheres in different directions. Diversity and plurality have asserted themselves incessantly through the established and enforced prisms. Today, acceptance of plurality in lieu of singularity of vision is the norm.

It is therefore imperative that we in India all the more cherish and celebrate plurality, whether of faiths or cultures or assertion of absence of faith in god or religion. That is the essence of true Indian-ness, which has for ages upheld the right of freedom of thought without postulating the triumph of one opinion over another, one single truth over all others. This is also the premise of the Indian Constitution's guarantee of civil rights. Denial of this freedom is the very anti-thesis of the great legacy of Indian civilisation. But then, this denial is being premised on the assertion of one truth as the single Truth, which is backed by the political dispensation that ironically seeks legitimacy in upholding ancient values!

After Partition, My Father Couldn't Find His Wife, But He Did Find Hope

The Wire, 15.08.2017

The Wire's #PartitionAt70 series brings a number of stories, through text and multimedia content that will attempt to draw a comprehensive picture of those weeks and months when entire geographies and histories changed forever.

I was born in 1937 or 38, in a tiny village in the Gujrat district of what is now Pakistan. No one, even in Pakistan, seems to have heard of the village Allaha, though it sits on my passport to this day. Our home was a nondescript one—a one-and-a-half room structure on one side of a dusty street; on the other side was a tall, white mansion-like habitat with a weathercock on top, which fascinated us kids for hours.

We moved to Delhi before the Partition—perhaps sometime around 1941. My father responded to the Quit India call and was put in a Multan prison for six months. My mother passed away perhaps in 1943 or 44, leaving behind five young children. My eldest sister, then 12 or 13, was withdrawn from school to look after her siblings. She never held it against us when we grew up and found our spaces in life.

A year or so before Partition, my father married his first cousin, his paternal uncle's daughter, back in Allaha.

The marriage procession consisted of the groom and his only son, me; the *bidai* procession added my new mother. It couldn't have been simpler.

On August 2 or 3, 1947, my grandmother landed at our home in Delhi and suggested that she and my mother go back to the village and escort the rest of the extended family to Delhi, and bring with them whatever savings they had. Father was aghast at the suggestion and appealed to grandma to hold on for another 12-13 days. After independence—to which he seriously thought he had a personal claim—had been celebrated, he would go there himself, instead of two women going on such a tough mission. Even at this stage, they did not suspect any great mishap in the offing. Grandma insisted and father had to give in.

The two women left Delhi for Allaha. That was the last we ever heard about them. The members of the family they had gone out to rescue, however, found their way to Delhi. Father was heartbroken. Understandably.

Then an incident brought him some hope. He was lightly educated, but was always a stickler for reason and logic for understanding and explaining any phenomenon; God had no place in his scheme. One day, he was whiling away his time on the broad street in old Delhi then called Faiz Bazaar, now Netaji Subhash Chandra Bose Road. A road show was on, where a boy lies on the floor "unconscious" and the master of the show keeps asking him about the problems facing members of the audience. Father was laughing away at the *tamasha* when suddenly the master asked the boy what his, father's, problem was. To his great astonishment, the boy spelt out his wife's name and announced that she was hiding in a building in our village, both of which he identified correctly without father even having to ask him to.

He was dumbstruck and his skepticism gave way to a faint hope—who knows, the boy might even be right. So he decided to take a chance. In around October, he travelled to Lahore and then on to the village. He was just short of six feet tall and, with a *kullah* (Afghani headgear), could easily pass off as Pathan. In Delhi, most of his friends in Darya Ganj, where we lived, were Muslims and he was familiar with their etiquette, besides knowing Urdu well. He faced no problem in looking up the particular building, but there was no trace of his young wife.

On his return, he wrote a short piece titled My visit to Pakistan, which was never published. But I remember some crucial parts of it. In Lahore he stayed with his Muslim friends from Faiz Bazar who had migrated to Pakistan. In the streets of Lahore, the real Pathans were shooting at street lights and in the air because there were no Hindus left to kill. His Muslim friends, who had given him shelter and support, risked their lives and properties for him. The slightest hint that they were knowingly hiding and supporting a kafir from India would give the Pathans the 'legitimate' right to wipe them out and plunder their house. But the truth remained with his hosts.

In the end, father couldn't find his wife. But he was able to reaffirm the one faith he had: that as often as not, human relations override political, national and even religious dividing lines.

Babur and the Masjid: First Reference to Ram Temple in Ayodhya Comes as Late as 1822

The Indian Express, 03.09.2019

A submission was made to the Supreme Court on August 28, 2019 by one party to the dispute that Babur never visited Ayodhya and makes no reference to Ram temple.

Well, Babur did visit the place in 1528 and records it twice in Babur Nama: "...stayed a few days... in order to settle the affairs of Aud" (medieval Persian texts' synonym for Ayodhya) and went out for a hunt. However, the submission is right on the second point. Babur makes no mention of a Ram, or any other temple there, nor that he had commissioned the construction of a mosque.

The first and primary evidence of the construction was inscribed on the outer and the inner walls of the mosque in a verse. Mir Baqi, Babur's noble, affirms in this verse that the mosque ("the alighting place of angels") was constructed by him under the express command of his master, the emperor. But he makes no mention of a temple, much less a Ram temple, having been made to yield the place for it. Babur himself makes no mention of either the mosque or of his command to the Mir.

The next bit of evidence comes from Abu'l Fazl, Akbar's

courtier-historian, in his *Ain-i Akbari*, where he records the length and breadth of Ayodhya and that "it is esteemed one of holiest places of antiquity... It is the residence of Ramchandra who in the *treta* age combined in his own person both the spiritual supremacy and kingly office". But he does not identify any site as his place of birth nor mention any temple dedicated to him, nor the existence of a mosque there.

If Babur as emperor and Abu'l Fazl as historian do not record the erection of a mosque at the site of a temple, they are not alone in their silence. None of Babur's descendants down to "the last Mughal" Bahadurshah Zafar, ever reminisces about it, not even the bigoted Aurangzeb, himself responsible for the demolition of Varanasi's Kashi Vishwanath and Mathura's Krishna temples and building of mosques in their place. Memory of his great ancestor's deed at Ayodhya should have filled him with joy, if he could locate it. Silence is all we hear. Silence also from the massive list of historians from the Mughal period—Muslims and Hindus, dogmatic and liberal. Silence also in enormous numbers of Hindi literary compositions, most astonishing being the silence of Goswami Tulsi Das. The great poet was a resident of Ayodhya and perhaps the greatest ever devotee of Ram, writing within five or six decades of the construction of the mosque; anger at the construction at the site of his Lord's birth itself and after destroying a temple dedicated to him would have driven him hopping mad. Not a word from him. Nor from anyone else.

The first concrete evidence of the identification of the site with Ram and the erection of Babari masjid comes from an 1822 document in the Persian language submitted to the Faizabad court by *darogha-i adalat*, Hafizullah. It says "Jama masjid, constructed by Emperor Babur at the janma asthan, that is at the site of birth of Ram, son of Raja Dasrat and is adjacent to the *rasoi* (kitchen) of Sita, wife of the aforesaid Ram"; it does not mention the existence of any temple at the site demolished to make way for the masjid. It is clear that the monument neither invited great celebration nor great lamentation nor even commemoration in any quarter.

In the 19th century, events took a fast turn and in some versions, a Ram temple came to be located at the site of the mosque, even as occasional violence began to erupt. But the version was still shaky enough in the 1860s when P Carnegy, writing about the Faizabad district, accepted it at one place attributing it to "locally affirmed sources", i.e popular tradition and wondering whether the temple was dedicated to Ram or to Buddha at another in the same book. By 1905, the tradition that the masjid had replaced a temple had found its way to the Fyzabad District Gazetteer of H R Neville, though it still spoke vaguely of "an ancient temple". In 1922, A S Beveridge, translator of Babur Nama, among other books, had firmly asserted that "presumably the order for building the mosque was given during Babur's stay in Aud (Ayodhya) in 934 A.H", and leaves none in doubt that it had "displaced at least in part an ancient Hindu shrine" though even she does not mention Ram. This is not part of the translation of the text but an Appendix U, she has added. It is a guess she has made and not a factual statement.

We can infer from the above that the first concrete historical evidence about the association of Lord Ram with the site under dispute comes nearly 300 years after the construction of the masjid. And as the discipline of history goes, the authenticity of evidence is greatly dependent on its proximity to the event it narrates. The later the evidence, the lower its reliability. How reliable would a statement first made in 2019 about an incident in 1719 be? There are other relevant variables too, but the chronology of the evidence is primary. Popular traditions are good subjects of study of the evolution of cultural norms; but these are poor testimony for judging the authenticity of a specific event in history.

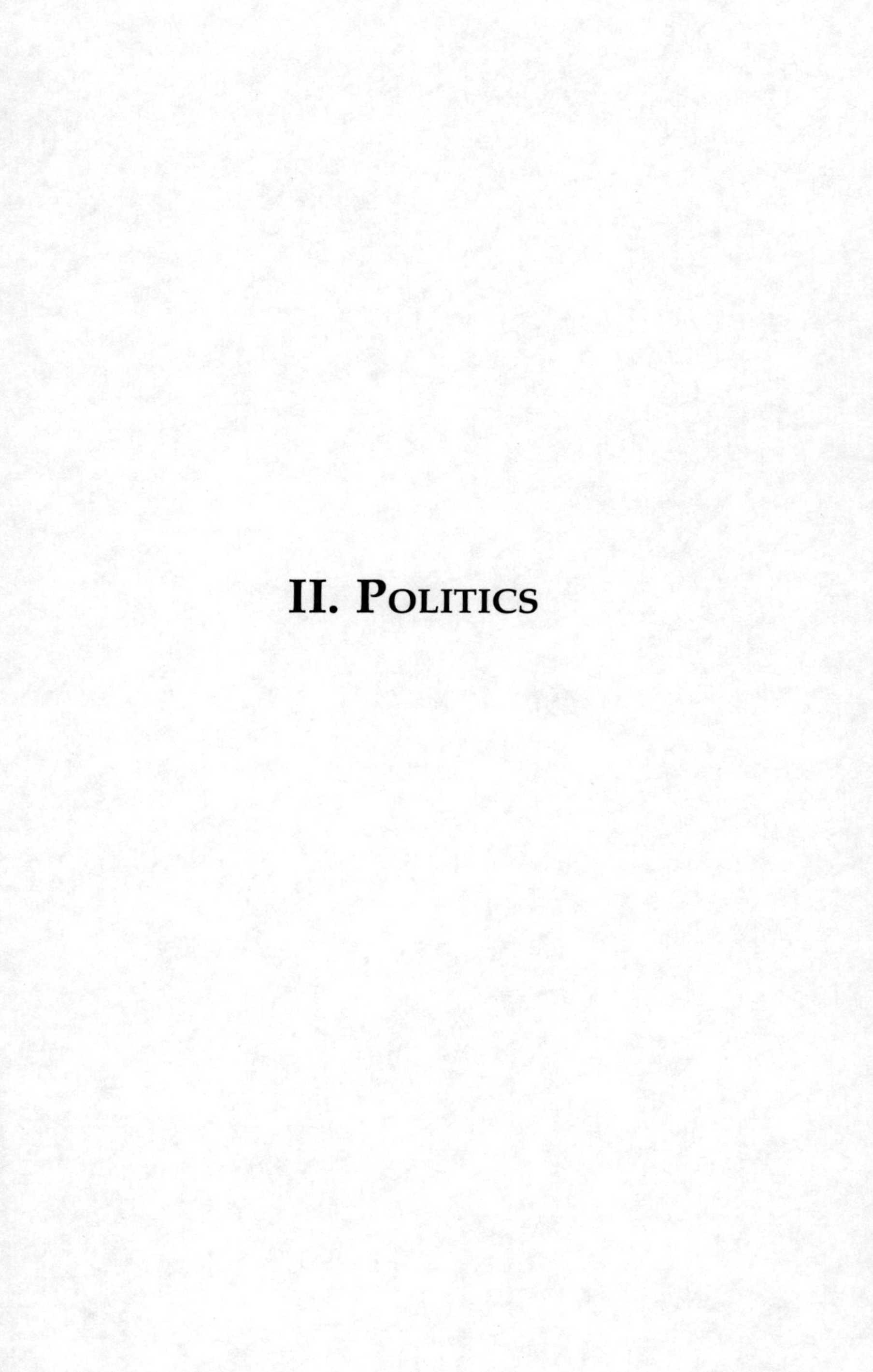

II. Politics

The Violence of Certainty

The Indian Express, 07.03.2017

The current spate of tension, including violence, on India's campuses is essentially reducible to a conflict between two notions of truth: the single Truth and a pluralist vision of truth whether the subject is nationalism or religion or any other. How attractive is the idea of Truth being absolute and pure and thus being the most powerful negation of untruth or falsehood! Indeed, if Truth is absolute, it must also be singular; conversely, untruth and falsehood must be multiple in nature. Was it always understood thus?

Time was when the notion of truth's singularity or plurality was at best academic. The forceful assertion of its singularity came with Judeo-Christian or Biblical monotheism. Judaism asserted the being of a single God as the absolute Truth and adherence to it essential for being a Jew. However, it was not a proselytising religion and did not impose this condition on others. That change came with Christianity. Jesus being the son of God, the ultimate Truth had been revealed to humanity through him in the Bible. Implicit in it was the falsehood of all other faiths, forms of belief, indeed all modes of thought of which there was a multitude.

All these came to be labelled "infidelity" with the embedded disapproval of lack of faith in that Truth. Since

Christianity was a proselytising religion, an irreconcilable conflict came to be posited between its single Truth and all the rest that were by their very nature falsehoods, a conflict of which the conclusion was foregone: Its ultimate and universal triumph over all that is false. The ultimate, universal triumph was also implicated in the notion of the Day of Judgment, by which day all of humanity would have turned to Christianity. Whether this triumph came through persuasion, persecution, temptation, use of state power etc. or a combination of all of these remained open-ended. But the monopoly of the Truth gave its owner unlimited power to tempt, punish, subjugate those whose loyalties lay elsewhere.

The notion of the absolute and therefore single Truth was inherited by Islam which announced that while partial truths had been revealed earlier through the agency of prophecy, Muhammad was the last in the line of prophets and therefore the single ultimate Truth was embedded in the Quran. Indeed, a synonym of God in Islam is the Truth (al-Haq). The slightest deviation from any word of the Quran was tantamount to *bida't* (heresy) and strictly unlawful. It also imbibed the concept of the Day of Judgment from Christianity and therefore the other attributes of the singularity of Truth and its inevitable triumph over falsehoods, termed kufr, with the same meaning and intensity as infidelity. On the Day of Judgment all humans would have turned to Islam. In Hindu as well as Jain and Buddhist philosophies, while debate on the nature of truth was frequent, it usually ended in the acceptance of at least plural versions of truth. Absence of a single foundational text or a prophet and above all, absence of the notion of the Day of Judgment, also contributed to this vision.

Interestingly, singularity of Truth was not confined to

religions alone. In a great twist of irony, the same premise underlay theology's and indeed religions' most strident ideological adversary—Marxism. For it too, all history is driven by one Truth, class struggle, and its inevitable universal triumph is written into it with the transition to the stage of socialism and ultimately communism. Class struggle is waged at various levels of persuasion, propagation etc., including but not exclusively through violence.

This indeed is the theory and a good deal of history has been shaped by it. The conflict and the violence unleashed by the tension between the Truth and falsehoods has been the cause of shedding untold amount of human blood and enormous destruction through history and has not ceased yet. But that is not history's only facet. There is an inverse side to it too. If the theory of the single Truth does not allow it to accept any space for an alternative view, the moderation wrought on it by history through the centuries has created that space. Space was created first by the emergence of divergent versions of the same Truth within the boundaries of each religion and ideology, including Marxism, and gradually the acceptance that alternate views, faiths and belief systems have survived all the violence unleashed upon them over such a long span of time. It is possible therefore that they are all somewhat better than utter falsehoods. Medieval Christian texts, for example, are teeming with denunciation of Muhammad as a false prophet; no longer. Within Islam too there has been questioning of the very legitimacy of prophethood, including Muhammad's, among several divergent views on the nature of Islam and its relationship with other religions. Marxism too has had a number of often competing versions during its lifetime and some of the giants among the "socialist" regimes were at more than an ideological war with one another.

Here is another irony in the making: As the religious and non-religious ideologies holding on to the notion of a single Truth have, over the centuries, moderated their thinking even if in varying degrees, we are now being driven into that street by the claimants to the one system of thought which had chosen its own distinctive path of pluralism. The Hindutva ideology of its current proponents, from V.D. Savarkar, M.S. Golwalkar to K.S. Sudarshan and Mohan Bhagwat, replicates the structure of the singularity of Truth with all its attendant violence. Perhaps this is the farthest Hinduism can go, or can be driven from its evolved pluralist vision. Interestingly, persuasion seems to be the weakest link in this drive: Use of power—state and administrative power including lure for compliance and punishment for defiance—is apparently the chief agency for this massive task of transformation.

Will it succeed? Well, history has witnessed even more massive transformations in the long term; it would be hard to predict success or failure with certainty. State power has effected several such processes in the past: The spread of Christianity, Islam and Marxism had intimate connections with it. On the other hand, the state that exists and operates in 21st century India is not the absolutist state that effected these processes and is unlikely to turn into one. That is one strong guarantee against the repetition of history.

The Pseudo Alternative

The Indian Express, 25.07.2016

The Sangh Parivar's claims to being the true repository of Indian history and culture become louder every time it wields political power. It announces purging history of all the impurities that colonialism, and the evils that Marxism, had introduced into it. It promises to rewrite history completely and produce nationalist history in all its pristine purity. However, whether during its earlier stint or during campaigns to capture power or now, it has gone wrong on historical facts. Narendra Modi located Taxila and the site of Alexander's "defeat" in Bihar while campaigning for elections to the Lok Sabha in 2014 while recently a former minister said celebrating Shivaji was necessary to avert the kind of devastation unleashed by Genghis Khan. The minister, of course, assumed that the destroyer bearing the surname Khan was unquestionably Muslim.

The former minister (of education to boot) was clearly unaware that Genghis Khan was not a Muslim and that he was, in fact, a scourge of the Muslim states in the region. His grandson, Hulagu, ransacked Baghdad and destroyed the Abbasid caliphate in 1258. We, in the profession of history, were looking forward to serious academic output that would be an alternative—like K.M. Munshi's multi-volume *History and Culture of the Indian People* or several works of R.C. Majumdar—to the much-maligned and highly overstated "colonialist-Marxist" paradigm. After six years of patronage between 1998 and 2004 and another period of over two years, all we have are outlandish claims that all manner of scientific, technological, surgical and philosophical knowledge originated in India with the Vedas.

Indeed, even this claim has been repeated since decades.

The contributions of ancient India, along with those of many other civilisations, Western and Eastern, Northern and Southern, in the realms of astronomy, mathematics, surgery and philosophy have long been recognised by professional historians around the world. The recent launch of a project by the ICHR to outline the scientific achievements of ancient India is welcome if it adds to the numerous volumes on the theme as well as the respected 50-year-old *Indian Journal of the History of Science*, published by the Indian National Science Academy. But, by itself, the project is unlikely to shake the earth. There is so little to look up to in the list of alternative history.

Far from a well-researched book, there is not even an article so far to lead us to that promised land of purist history writing and understanding of culture.

There is good reason for this. The discipline has long moved beyond the framework the Parivar is keen on deploying. History driven solely by the ruler's religious identity was the most significant change colonial historiography effected to the multifaceted explorations of the discipline in ancient and medieval India. Historical time, before that, was unfamiliar with the famous tripartite division of Hindu-Muslim-British periods introduced by James Mill's in 1818; some decades later, Elliot and Downson, in their massive eight-volume *History of India as Told by its Own Historians*, reinforced the deadly effect of this scheme. The intent of the effort was never concealed: "To teach the bombastic babus the great relief British rule had brought them from the tyranny of the Muslim rulers"—this was divide and rule in its perfect form.

Post-Independence, Indian historians of all hues, including Marxists, challenged the assumptions of colonial historiography and new perspectives began to evolve. The major departure was to expand the space and scope of history from the rulers and their courts to the ground level—peasants, artisans and later on the "subalterns" as well—in order to give a multi-dimensional focus to history where religious identity, not of the rulers alone, but also of social and political groups counted as one of the dimensions. The rise and fall of dynasties began to get explained, not in terms of the strong or weak ruler phenomenon, but in a complex set of social, economic, ideational and institutional conflicts and symbioses. Themes of history also underwent radical expansion and that continues at a breathtaking pace: The history of gender relations, of ecology, mindscapes embedded in literature, paintings, folklore, history of the notions of time and space, histories of attitudes towards death and life, sexuality, family, notions of masculinity and femininity, history of perceptions of the past, the list is unending and constantly growing.

Such history, written from any perspective, is incapable of being reduced to a model of Hindu-Muslim antagonism driven entirely by the ruler's religious identity. That is the Sangh Parivar's problem. Even as it hopes to divide and rule by pitting the gaurakshaks against the beef eaters, the Parivar's agenda of rewriting history and bringing back the glories of ancient India remains a pipe-dream. It's not for nothing that there has not been a single book or even an article from its historians that has been under discussion on any platform, right-wing or left- wing, over the past few decades.

Perhaps the Parivar is aware of this and has opted for rewriting history at the school textbooks level where the simplistic colonial, Mill-Elliot-Dowson kind of history can be reproduced for young minds. This also stems from the training at the RSS shakhas where such history is, ironically, passed on as "nationalist" par excellence. This is what Murli Manohar Joshi did as the minister of education in the last BJP-led NDA government. A supplementary strategy is to "rewrite" history at the local-level where the old syncretic legacies can be purged to yield either exclusive images or, more profitably, images of conflict. This can be done—and is being done—without drawing much attention, although there has been no shortage of resources, as well as patronage, for the endeavour. There is help from the "left-liberal" historians too for this: Their nearly exclusive preoccupation with grand entities, whether empires or peasant uprisings or grand "transitions" and neglect of regional, especially local history has left space for those who have their sights set on it.

What's Left?

The Indian Express, 21.04.2015

The story we heard back in the late 1950s was that Gamal Abdel Nasser, legendary president of Egypt, was visiting India, and Jawaharlal Nehru held a reception for him. Nehru was personally introducing Nasser to several invitees, Hiren Mukherjee among them. Nehru introduced him too, as the communist MP. He saw the unasked question in Nasser's eyes—"Communist MP?"—and answered it: "Mr President, you have put your communists in prison, I have put them in Parliament." Implied in the answer was that there are different ways of making communists irrelevant to a functioning democracy.

Not quite, though. Both Indian democracy and Indian communists have shown remarkable resilience to survive and flourish, with all the ups and downs inherent in the process. Their adaptability to the conditions of what the communists still classify almost derisively as bourgeois democracy is testimony enough, even for those not quite their sympathisers. Yet, the fact that a crisis of existence stares them in the face is one of the most important and honest admissions of the CPM's just-concluded party congress. The party is seeking a way out in the leadership of one of its most promising leaders, Sitaram Yechury.

As president of the JNUSU in 1977-78, Yechury was

quite a terror for members of the university's Academic Council (AC). He never raised his voice, never uttered one word that could be objected to and was, in fact, polite to a fault. The terror was the AC meetings in which he raised and argued on issues relating to students for 10 hours; all other issues of would be disposed of in a half-hour!

The ability to present his argument with cogency, clarity and force has served him and his party well. Once in a while when one gets to hear him intervene in the Rajya Sabha debates, the affection and admiration for him comes back. It came back when he opened his acceptance of the general secretary's post with the statement: "This [party] congress is the congress of the future." He has also assured the audience of the party's turnaround.

Is this mere rhetoric, or is there substance to the assertions? It remains an open question, even though Yechury does have a vision. His emphasis on countering neoliberal economic policies, rather than taking on capitalism itself, the threat of social cleavages being followed as a well-thought-out strategy by the Narendra Modi government, and his concern for the declining support for his party and its ideals, especially among the youth, underline his vision. He is aware that on one hand, the world today lives under the supreme dominance of capitalism with its alternative decimated; on the other, the world is in ferment as seldom before. If the neoliberal economic regime is increasingly spiralling all wealth to the top 1 per cent around the world, theoretical as well as political challenges to it are also growing in all corners. Besides the basic questions being raised by Noam Chomsky, Thomas Piketty, Slavoj Zizek and others, and the massive protests staged in the Western world over the years, alternative regimes have been experimented with in Iceland, Venezuela, Uruguay and more recently in Greece, with Spain threatening to follow.

Clearly, ever evolving modes of thought, strategies and forms of mobilisation to gain political space in India is the chief challenge before the new team in the party's politburo. The AAP has demonstrated that staging huge rallies at the Ramlila Ground in Delhi is not always the best way of mobilisation; dedicated volunteers' close and constant contact with the people is a more telling form. In some ways, the BJP also invented, under Modi's leadership, massive mobilisation through a deluge of publicity never seen before. Two alternatives to the existing practices of political parties, both extremely successful, because some different thinking was invoked. The situation calls for new modes of thought and planning.

But the CPM's target is not and should not merely be mobilisation to win elections; much more is at stake, for itself and for the nation. Yechury has rightly laid equal stress on keeping the social fabric of India alive, which is being ripped apart by the present regime. Ask a school child what characterised the British colonial regime and pat would come the answer, "divide and rule". Thinking back, the colonialists seemed to have been utter novices in this arena; the real masters are the Sangh Parivar, with diverse roles assigned to all its constituents in the government and outside. The communists have the great advantage over other parties in that caste or religious identities are not central to their mode of thinking and social and political operations. They can and do operate outside of either the "Hindu-Muslim bhai bhai" or "Hindu-Muslim enemies" syndrome.

There seems to be promise in Yechury's early response to his election that the time has come to go beyond making intelligent statements and passing resolutions on issues of grave importance to the nation. It is time to truly connect with the people who matter to it. The AAP has shown that it is possible to do so within an amazingly short period of time and practically without organisational backing. The CPM would be ill-advised to imitate the AAP mode. But it must realise that the future Yechury talked about demands hard rethinking and even harder ground work. We, sitting on the fences, can only hope for the best—a hope that is not untouched by some apprehension.

Left, Right, AAP

The Indian Express, 14.02.2015

Has Arvind Kejriwal altered the paradigm of India's politics? What rubbish, many of us would say. Politicians of this brand come and go and are soon forgotten. One serious charge that is constantly levied against the Aam Aadmi Party in general and Kejriwal in particular is that they lack a clear ideological perspective to guide their actions, which then acquire an ad hoc character. And the charge does not originate in hostility to them, even as it is not even firmly denied by them.

But then the charge itself arises from certain ideas about what constitutes ideology. We have grown up with ideology being cast in terms of binary opposites of class, gender and, in India specifically, caste. Its purported "scientific" schema was laid down by Marx and Engels. In this schema, society, economy, state, politics, culture, religion—everything—imbibed a class character in a general context of irreconcilable class antagonism. Change, in this scenario, could occur only with the overthrow of one class by another and the replacement of an entire structure dominated by one class with an alternative one. There was no shared space in between. It had a sense of deliberate abolition of the past, as it were. The French Revolution was the first such moment of transition, which "abolished feudalism" through a law passed by the Assemblée Nationale one fine morning in August 1789. The 20th century saw several more changes which overthrew either feudal or bourgeois regimes. The socialist revolution of Russia was to mark the arrival of the penultimate stage of class antagonism, prior only to the end of all class struggle as humanity marched into the stage of communism, which would eradicate all trace of class difference among human beings. A dream-like prospect.

If the failure of the Soviet experiment does not nullify the concept of class difference in existing societies, it points to alternative modes of resolving social and other tensions. The concept of liberal democracy, which has virtually come to be equated with periodic, multi-party free and fair elections or representative democracy—very inadequate, in effect, for meeting the aspirations of the common masses—is a working alternative, and the only one available at present. The other option is to boycott it and wage revolutionary class war outside its framework, an option no longer viable.

It is true that the working of liberal democracy has almost universally been characterised by a gap between its promises and its delivery. The promises made to "we the people" in idealistic constitutions drafted in grand constitutional assemblies, made up of the most highly educated elites, have been denied to the people in real life. We have now reached a stage where about 80 individuals own half the world's wealth and they have acquired it largely in the most advanced democratic set-ups.

Yet, the option of delivering the promises made by the same liberal democratic constitutions is opening up. Several experiments in Latin American states and societies, in Iceland and, most recently, in Greece have demonstrated the feasibility of looking after the interests of the poor and the downtrodden—and of the ecology—within the available framework of "democracy". In other words, the ideology that has guided these experiments is redefining Marxism itself by drawing it away from the premise of irreconcilable class antagonism. The objective here is not to do away with the capitalist system but to compel it to fulfil the promises made by the "bourgeois" constitutions. Honesty of purpose seems to have replaced the ideological commitment to class antagonism.

This appears to be the guiding perspective of the AAP. It is not as if Kejriwal and his friends have sat down to deliberate these issues, even though it has eminent intellectuals steeped in the social sciences, such as Yogendra Yadav, Anand Kumar, Kamal Mitra Chenoy, Rajmohan Gandhi and others, in the higher echelons of the party leadership. But then, perspectives do not evolve through deliberations among intellectuals. They evolve through interactions with the people and a deliberate as well as intuitive understanding of their problems and aspirations. It would be interesting to investigate how many epoch-making leaders, like Mahatma Gandhi and Nelson Mandela, developed their perspectives by reading learned treatises. As recent exciting experiments in direct democracy, in Iceland and earlier Venezuela, have demonstrated, perspectives traverse many diverse and complex terrains as they evolve.

Thus, what the AAP is experimenting with is not a grand theory of overthrow or revolution but one of enlarging the public space within the existing structures. It is not premised on upheavals of one sort or another, but on an incremental claiming of rights that have, in practice, been denied to the common people, the aam aadmis.

Will this experiment evaporate into thin air? There is no guarantee that it will survive the expected onslaught of vested interests. But there is no guarantee that it will succumb to threats or temptations held out by vested interests either. Kejriwal has always laid stress on the sincerity of intentions and shown no sign of wavering from them, although it is too early to decide and power has the habit of corrupting. But if it is important to keep one's scepticism alive, especially when it comes to leaders, it is equally important to grant them honesty and commitment to a cause until such time as they belie it. It is the simple principle of "innocent until proven guilty".

But the success of the AAP experiment in Delhi will, even if not in full measure but substantially, in Nehru's memorable words, galvanise other areas of public and political life in India. It is easy to envisage its cascading effect if it works out. That is its real message. That is our hope.

Fashioning a Vision of the Future

The Hindu, 14.01.2014; Updated: 13.05.2016

Very legitimate concerns have lately been expressed whether the new phenomenon on India's political horizon, the Aam Aadmi Party, has evolved any theoretical perspectives on how to engage with the massive and complex problems of the vast country. Aside from the manifold issues of foreign policy, relations with neighbours, problems of caste, religion, communalism etc., what is its vision for the future economic growth of the nation? On the face of it, the AAP leadership does not appear to have given thought to these and does not appear to have a cogent, comprehensive theory to guide its actions.

Yet, all actions do have some theoretical perspectives implicit in them, irrespective of the actors' conscious formulation—or even awareness—of these. What perspectives inform the AAP's recent chaotic actions?

One major theoretical presence during much of the twentieth century was the Marxist theory which postulated social and economic transformation from one stage of development to another—from feudalism to capitalism to socialism, etc. Each transformation would be complete and comprehensive, replacing all preceding structures of the economy, polity, even modes of thought and behaviour; there were no shared spaces between one and another.

Yet, history has demonstrated the existence of common spaces and the "transformation" from one "stage" to another was highly qualified by the continuing presence of older "structures" into their replacement. One of the decrees passed by the Assemblée nationale in Paris on 11 August, 1789, in the wake of the French Revolution, brazenly announced that "feudalism stood abolished from today", heralding the onset of the bourgeois regime. Yet, as several historians have shown, so much of the preceding "feudalism" had survived that the term "Revolution" had lost a great deal of its sheen. In our own living memory, the Soviet Revolution in 1917 substituted socialism for the bourgeois "stage" in its totality; yet, after seven long decades of absolute dominance, socialism could not eliminate its predecessor which had obviously survived underneath with enough power to overthrow it in one swift move in 1990-91.

Therefore, a different theory had to evolve, one that drew us away from binary oppositions. Interestingly, several recent experiments in Latin America in theory and in practice are exciting precisely because these modify both capitalism and Marxism. If Marxism posits social progress through contradictions, necessitating the elimination of one mode of production to ensure the installation of another, capitalism premises its (and society's) growth on maximisation of private profit, never mind society's urgent needs—especially the needs of those with minimal purchasing power—and the need to limit exploitation of natural resources to preserve ecological balance. Thus, when Venezuela placed an obligation on its big entrepreneurs to produce what the poor of the country required for subsistence even as the entrepreneurs earned legitimate profits, and when Ecuador granted a constitutional right to its ecology, the "contradiction" between capitalism and socialism was being modified. Socialism here did not predicate the abolition of capitalism and capitalism could no longer walk the free street of unfettered exploitation of natural resources for maximisation of profit.

"Bio-socialism" is the beautiful term they have coined for this scenario. Representative democracy is also being complemented with participatory democracy in several countries to the extent of forcing governments to rescind laws already passed or decisions already taken.

In other words, the existing institutions and systems need not be replaced by alternative sets of institutions and systems; these can be deployed for meeting society's needs from the bottom upwards. The promises of liberal democracy, which had been defeated by the unfettered and unregulated growth of capitalism, as Noam Chomsky and several other thinkers have been arguing of late, can be met from within the system by reworking it. The urgent need at the moment is to implement the promises made by many democratic constitutions around the world instead of seeking to overthrow these bodies.

Deliberation Needed

The AAP leaders clearly have not sat down to deliberate on these issues; but their slogans and actions have the appearance of holding the Constitution and institutions to their promises to the people of India, something along the lines of what's happening in Latin America. When the movement started some two years ago at Ramlila Ground, the frightened political class first denounced it as a challenge to the venerable democratic institutions and then sought to sabotage it by making promises it had no intention of fulfilling. "Laws are made in Parliament and not in Ramlila Ground" was its war cry, typically seeking to mislead public opinion. "These unelected and unelectable men are insulting the temple of democracy, i.e. Parliament," screamed leaders of the government and the Opposition in unison, even as for weeks and months together Parliament's routine functioning was disrupted by them. Anna Hazare and Arvind Kejriwal had never sought the substitution of Ramlila Ground for Parliament, but demanded that it pass a Bill in accordance with the will of the people. Mr. Kejriwal and his comrades have taken oath to honour the Constitution of India, not to abolish it and they are seeking to embed all their actions within the framework of given laws and institutions, but with a turn that had been ignored, even denied for so long. Clearly, the same institutions can be turned into the facilitators of or the stumbling blocks for society's progress. That seems to be the perspective at work.

How far will this take us? Some good distance, yes, but soon the demand for a conscious and clearer understanding of the nature of society and its aspirations and the modes of meeting them would certainly become acute. It is clear that any given model picked from somewhere and blandly enforced here would defeat itself. A long-term and sound vision alone can lead us to that distant land called the future. We cannot quite arrive there by kicking stones that lie as we walk; a clearer path needs to be laid out.

Making it 'for the People' Again

The Hindu, 13.10.2012; Updated: 18.10.2016

The one significant question being thrown us by the India Against Corruption (IAC) movement is this: is the movement for or against the country's much revered democracy? The answer, as often in questions relating to society or politics, is neither a clear yes nor no. It is anti-democratic in as much as democracy has become the equivalent of the holding of elections and the forming of governments. Once elections have been held and governments formed, any questioning of the rights—or, more important, the legitimacy—of any act of our elected representatives or of the elected governments, except through the due processes of law, is immediately pronounced anti-democratic. There are institutions and provisions within the democratic structures available to citizens to express their dissent, we are assured; any movement outside of these structures itself becomes illegal, and therefore illegitimate.

But the institutions and structures also have a life and a mutable character. When these have turned, or have been perceived to have turned, into fortresses for the defence of the rights and decisions of those who have been elected and those who find favour with them, never mind through what manner or means, and when these rights and decisions are perceived to be in conflict with the very lives of those who have elected them, the legitimacy, if not strictly the legality, of the institutions and structures lends itself to grave questioning. Let us remember that the declaration of the Emergency in 1975 was perfectly legal; it was its dubious legitimacy that led to the defeat of the ruling party in the elections of 1977.

Today, once again, there are serious doubts about the legitimacy of the whole system of governance which has spawned unforeseen corruption and, above all, an economy that increasingly concentrates wealth at the very thin upper crust leaving the "99 per cent" to fend for themselves. Corruption, while being an issue in itself, is indeed the instrument of the implementation of economic policies that have created, and are constantly creating fissures between the "1 per cent" and the "99 per cent"; and corruption is not merely monetary in nature; it is corruption of the whole system of governance that is at stake. Corruption of the electoral process which sends a third of elected leaders with self-declared heinous crimes like murder, kidnapping, rape and the rest to virtually every Assembly and the Lok Sabha. The judiciary has also been shown to be less than lily white. The democratic institution of periodic elections offers no way out for those at the receiving end, for periodic recirculation of power among the political parties has only brought a periodic redistribution of wealth among them and their cohorts. They are all quite happy with it.

Not Exclusive

Indeed, what is happening in India is not exclusive to it; in some ways the redistribution of wealth and its concentration at the upper end is happening in a major chunk of the planet we inhabit, following the same economic doctrines. The forms of popular resistance to it are also similar—outside the framework of the legal and institutional systems. The slogan "We are the 99 per cent" originated in New York as did the "Occupy Wall Street" movement, although it did not impact the U.S. polity substantially. But growing awareness of the inequities of the paths of growth around the world is in itself a significant phenomenon denoting a restlessness that is often a precursor to encompassing metamorphoses. Even now, a different regime of economy is being experimented within parts of Latin America, to an extent in Brazil, but especially in Venezuela.

Is IAC then seeking an overthrow of the system of democracy that has evolved in India over the past 60-odd years? At any rate, is it possible at all to do that? Not quite; neither of these. The fact that a branch of IAC, led by Arvind Kejriwal, will participate in elections and seek the popular mandate to govern, should put paid to any suspicion on that score.

Right from the days of Anna Hazare's fast at Jantar Mantar last year, the loud cry being heard was that he is undermining the country's hallowed democratic institutions, although he would have found the competition to do so with elected representatives very hard to win. Not allowing Parliament to function when you do not have a majority does not quite enhance the spirit of democracy, and lest we forget, no party has patented an exclusive right to this practice. IAC's actions on the streets and in public places, often verging on the absurd, highlight the conflict that has got entrenched between the institutions of governance and the aspirations of the people, contrary to the very premise of democracy which emphasises a symbiosis between the two. The movement is a clarion call to the system as a whole to redefine the polity and the economy to restore the symbiosis so crucial to an orderly functioning; it is a call for reforming from within rather than the threat of an overthrow.

Waking the Higher Education Elephant

The Indian Express, 30.06.2009

The enormous significance of the Nehruvian vision for higher education in India is now coming home to us,as India earns its niche in the 21st-century world. With all its many shortcomings and failures,it still remains true that at the higher level of teaching and research in almost all branches, be it natural sciences,medicine,social sciences or literature, Indian universities have enabled their students to find placement in the best of institutions anywhere in the world. Yet, there is still a very long way to go.

Having taught history for 44 years at Delhi University's Hindu College (where incidentally Kapil Sibal was briefly my younger department colleague some 40 years ago) and JNU, I can perhaps claim a little intimacy with some of the problems that inhabit higher education. Chief among these is not financial constraints: it is the problem of resistance to experimentation oneself,coupled with an even greater reluctance to let with students engage in it. In other words,the chief problem is intellectual inertia. Thus,despite everything, teaching and research in India has not produced one overarching concept or theory,or one invention that has led to a paradigm shift in virtually any branch of knowledge or, for that matter, in governing humanity's daily life. Our systems are too hidebound for that. G. Parthasarathi, JNU's founding Vice-Chancellor, didn't share this narrowness;

his vision,to allow its students and faculty precious space for freedom and intellectual adventure, still survives in patches, and is what has earned it such high respect.

Yet, even in institutions like JNU, the space was highly constricted and seems to have become more so over time. Theoretically, for example, a student can seek admission to any discipline in JNU irrespective of one's previous disciplinary background, if one is able to clear the admission test; and there have been cases where such boundaries were indeed crossed. But on the whole the ratio of such cross-discipline admissions would not exceed a fraction of a per cent. The boundaries get tighter once admission has been given. The faculties are mainly uni-disciplinary, as are the courses; and reaching out to courses in other disciplines is tightly controlled. Yet, whenever these controls are relaxed, the results are spectacular. Let me cite two such examples.

Ramya Srinivasan was a young lecturer in English literature in Miranda House when she sought admission to the PhD course in history at JNU with the proposal to work on the evolution of the many legends of Rani Padmini of Chittor over several centuries and in different regions. She could not convince the Centre for Historical Studies that, given her background in English literature, she would be able to deal with the subject with competence. Luckily, the Centre for English was more relaxed and admitted her, to be jointly supervised by Professor Minakshi Mukherjee (later Professor J.G.V. Prasad) and me. Today, an associate professor of history at a premier university in the US, she is the author of an outstanding book on the subject, that dexterously combines her expertise in literary criticism and historical contextualisation. Sumit Ganguli was doing his Master's in medieval history and wanted to opt for a course in human rights. Asked the faculty: what has human rights got to do with medieval history? But somehow he got permission. He pursued the subject further—coming back to Chennai as UNHRC's representative.

Thus, just a little leeway in letting students go beyond the strict rules can produce competence of very high calibre. Our students at the university level deserve more, rather than less, such flexibility. And this flexibility needs to be institutionalised.

But a prime requisite of greater flexibility is the teachers' constant engagement in updating as well as widening their own knowledge. Failure to do so,even for just three-to-five years,can leave one a long distance behind,given the rapidity with which knowledge in each discipline is changing. With the very impressive improvement in teachers' salaries recently,it is the libraries and the laboratories that call for immediate and focused attention. This,and some system of rewards for excellence—which necessarily also implies absence of rewards for the laggards. Nothing damages a system more than its inability to distinguish between energy and lethargy. It is a shame that we do not have a mechanism in place even for ensuring regular taking of one's classes,much less of updating one's knowledge. It is hard to imagine greater inhumanity than for a teacher to pass on outdated knowledge to one's unsuspecting students.

With Sibal in charge, expectations are high, hoping for radical change. It will be a great tribute to Nehru's vision to raise the system once again to the stature which he had accorded it. Raising of teachers' salaries is one major welcome step in that direction; the stage is ready for the many others.

Break the Mould, End the Siege

The Indian Express, 24.03.2018

Ideas Series: The Minority Space

Two pieces carried recently in these columns—Harsh Mander's 'Sonia, sadly' (March 17) and Ramachandra Guha's response 'Liberals, sadly' (March 20)—have set off a larger discussion on democracy, majoritarianism and how these shape the space for minorities. While Mander wrote about the growing invisibility and marginalisation of Muslims in the public-political sphere in the current moment, for Guha the problem is the surrendered possibilities of Muslim political leadership and social reform. The debate continues.

Harsh Mander ('Sonia, sadly', March 17) and Ramachandra Guha ('Liberals, sadly', March 20) have both expressed legitimate concerns about the situation of Indian Muslims in the current socio-political scenario and understandably each has a variant diagnosis and therefore a variant solution. Without going into the merits of either, I suggest that the analysis of the problem demands that we traverse a little longer distance into history and take a more general view.

The two major proponents of the two-nation-theory, V.D. Savarkar and M.A. Jinnah, also shared a political strategy, that is of creating a siege mentality for their respective communities, the Hindus and the Muslims, each imagined as exclusive, internally cohesive and facing a threat from the other. If Savarkar's support to divisive politics was halted because an alternative vision of Mahatma Gandhi and the Congress had an immensely wider social acceptance, Jinnah was largely spared the travails of an alternative even though it was not completely absent. What has, however, survived the Partition is the siege mentality, pervasive among Indian Muslims and now being laboriously cultivated among Hindus.

The mentality among the Muslims has been reinforced by almost every political and social grouping around. The association of guilt for the Partition, thrust on the manifold more numerous Muslims who stayed back than those who went away, is never allowed to pass into silence. The single driving force of the RSS and its extensive parivar is intense hostility, indeed hatred, for the Muslims, with frequent violent expression as communal riots, pushes the community into defensive isolation. This has come electorally handy for the Congress: Vote for us is the price of protection; else, see the RSS sword hanging on your head?

The sangh parivar is, especially under the present political leadership, assiduously carrying out M.S. Golwalkar's mission of disenfranchising the Muslims by seeking to consolidate the 80 plus per cent Hindu vote-bank, adding a massive dose to the Muslims' defensiveness and insularity. The leadership of the Muslim community, largely abandoned into the hands of imams, could only make itself indispensable by highlighting the siege that had entrapped the community and suggesting that the way out is by going back to a more puritanical Islam with all its attendant rituals, including its supposed dress codes and issuing the most absurd fatwas on the most absurd issues.

The liberal Muslims too have only weakly driven

home to the community the challenges of the 20th and 21st century and the need for meeting these with contemporary modes of thinking and mobilisation of its own internal resources alongside what the state has to offer. They have been mainly concerned with the alleged decline of Urdu, the denial of government jobs and educational opportunities; the responsibility for the backwardness of the community remains entirely outside of itself. In other words, everyone, including the community, has contributed to the strengthening of the single Muslim identity, especially vulnerable to political exploitation both by the "secular" parties as much as by the communalist parivar.

It is not as if no voices of dissent within the community and therefore, challenge to these dominant forces have ever been raised. Besides individuals, the most telling instance of activism on its behalf was the Shah Bano case when strong voices of men like Arif Muhammad Khan and numerous Muslim women were getting a growing public audience and approval for the judgment delivered by the Supreme Court in favour of the abandoned lady and warning the government against overriding it. But the political leadership, at the helm of which stood the impeccably secular leader Rajiv Gandhi, was persuaded that the Muslim community could not be trusted with any voice other than that of the imams. The fear of losing the Muslim vote if the imams were ignored lurked in the background. A great symbolic opportunity to break the siege was lost. The consequences of it are still with us. Succumbing to the imams did not fetch Rajiv Gandhi the Muslim votes, but it gave social acceptance to the sangh charge of minority appeasement and, far more than Advani's rath yatra, boosted the political fortunes of the BJP. Incidentally, succumbing to the Muslim clergy has never yielded political dividends to any party: The CPM too found it to its own cost when the Buddhadeb Bhattacharjee government in West Bengal did not waste even minutes throwing out Taslima Nasreen from Kolkata on the eve of elections when half a dozen little-known Muslims demanded it. Her ousting did not bring Muslim votes to the party. Conclusive proof, if it was needed, that Muslims do not vote as per the diktats of their clergy. But the political class goes by the stereotypes it has itself created: No proofs have any relevance here.

The problem then is not of wearing skull caps and burkas, or of Rahul Gandhi visiting temples on the eve of elections or visiting all places of worship all the year round. It is one of breaking the single mould into which the entire community has been cast over the past hundred odd years and this mould is one of siege. When we speak of the Hindu community, we immediately highlight the innumerable divisions within, caste divisions in particular, but the Muslims have just one identity, never mind the numerous differences and stratifications among them and the multiple times they have demonstrated these. The inherited single mould gets reinforced again and again by the addition of a sense of fear and insecurity which has been part of the deal handed out to the community and for breaking out of which the community has shown rather feeble energy, some instances notwithstanding.

The endeavour to break out has to be led from within the community, boldly taking risks and standing up for the community and for India. Not easy, especially when a militant majoritarian threat is looming large on it, but when were social transformations easy?

Is A New India Rising?

The Hindu, 14.01.2020

The tsunami of protests across the length and breadth of the country has several fascinating facets. Are there any significant pointers in it?

First and foremost, these are clearly the civil society's autonomous protests, devoid of any organic links with any political party. Barring issuing some statements in support or occasional visits by leaders to a protest site, even political parties have kept themselves at a distance from these protests. Underlying the autonomy is perhaps an unarticulated feeling that the issues evoking the protests go beyond electoral battles; that these concern the very life and blood of society's future. There is also an unarticulated assumption that the solution lies beyond the ken of one or the other political party or indeed all parties together. Therefore, reliance on a party or a group, any group, might end up in diversion, which often becomes equivalent of betrayal. The one possible link with political parties is perhaps a potential realisation by them that they might be left aside by the people if they keep the distance intact—a case of people leading the parties instead of the other way round.

The Power of Resistance

A consequence of civil society's direct involvement is that it is refusing to buy the current regime's divisive Hindu-Muslim formula. This formula has already fetched the National Democratic Alliance two terms in Parliament but seems to have hit a wall. Resistance began with society's response to uncalled-for police brutality on students in Jamia Millia Islamia and Aligarh Muslim University. And soon the chief target of resistance became the Citizenship Amendment Act—National Register of Citizens—National Population Register strategy devised by the regime to pit the Muslim community against the rest. The wide-ranging and unrelenting participation of people from all groups in the protests is clear enough signal of society's refusal to fall for it. Interesting also is the Muslim community's refusal to fall for the strategy of making their identity dichotomous with their Indian identity; the Muslims have instead sought to assert their religious identity in full concert with their Indian national identity by flaunting both at the same time, which in any case is far truer than the one which counterposes the two.

The resistance from the students is an amazing aspect even as it is wise to remind ourselves that their community has been the most energetic element in India's various resistance movements—and for that matter elsewhere around the world, whether in the anti-colonial struggles in Asia, Africa and Latin America, or the anti-Vietnam war protests in the U.S. Their protests have also grown in dimensions from repression in universities to the regime's hitherto successful Divide and Rule policy and its latest version encapsulated in the CAA-NRC-NPR. Neither has the government's incessant attempts to convince them of the honesty of its purpose, which could also be called brainwashing, failed to persuade them, nor has the repeated assertion by Home Minister Amit Shah of not budging an inch deterred them.

One of the most vociferous charges made against the government has been its grave attempt to prevent students and others from questioning it by simply branding such people as "anti-nationals" of which various equivalents have been newly minted: "anti-Modi", "anti-Hindu", "Urban Naxal". The government has also unleashed a barrage of filthy abuse and threats on social media through a highly organised IT machine under the BJP's control. A good segment of the media—now being called 'Modia'—has also pitched in with its aggressive campaign of malice against anyone with the mildest of doubts against the government's extravagant claims.

Yet, all this could not crush the spirit of questioning, especially on campuses, repression notwithstanding. The examples are now beyond count: there are protests in Hyderabad University, Jadavpur University, Banaras Hindu University, the Indian Institutes of Technology, Aligarh Muslim University, Jamia Millia Islamia, Delhi University and even in some of the safe and secure private universities. Jawaharlal Nehru University is an outstanding instance of standing up to repression for over four years now. Repression in any case is not the most durable of all forms of governance; this is one of history's abiding lessons. The wider society is waking up to the limits of repression as state policy and responding.

Quality of Leadership

One of the most endearing aspects of the current wave of protests is the exemplary quality of leadership displayed by students from the underprivileged social strata. Kanhaiya

Kumar has become a national figure thanks largely to the Modi government's atrocious handling of his "crime" which enabled him to demonstrate his extraordinary oratorical skill and his clear-headed perspectives to put forward his case with almost devastating ease. It is fascinating that the extempore slogan he raised on the JNU campus for "azadi" on his release from jail in 2016 has now become the national war cry for students and the youth. But he is one among innumerable other emerging leaders of student movements across the country. It is heartwarming to see young women taking up verbal, and now even physical, challenges to articulate their feelings and thoughts lucidly, fearlessly and forcefully. JNU Students' Union president Aishe Ghosh has once again occupied premier space on this front, thanks again to the mishandling by the Modi regime. One also comes across a large number of such promising student leaders on local channels speaking in their local language. This is where one sees promise of a new generation refusing to buy any "line" of any party but laying down its own terms for the country's future discourse. The conflict is no longer between the BJP and the Opposition parties' vote banks; it is now firmly situated between the BJP government and the people of India.

Democracy as We Know It is Inherently Flawed and Needs Fixing

The Wire, 20.07.2019

Democracy evolved as an integral part of the world's project of "modernity", even as some of its early forms had been practiced in different civilisations of the ancient world. The "modern" democracy evolved as part of a package of the individual's rights in opposition to the absolute, divine right of the medieval monarch legitimised by theology.

A new economic regime, centred on the factory in lieu of land which released human labour from being tied to the land and made it mobile, was another facet of evolving individual freedoms, which took centuries and varied enormously from region to region and time to time. But it ended up becoming a universal aspiration. This is democracy in brief.

The most developed form of democracy thus far is the practice of regular multi-party "free and fair" elections which has come to be accepted as its sine qua non. The underlying assumption is that each person exercises her franchise by her individual will and the majority of such "wills" exercised in favour of one of competing parties gives it the right to rule over the entire population on behalf of the "majority".

Simple. But that is also one of its major flaws. To begin

with, 50% + 1 vote is not weighty enough to give it such dominance over its rival with 50% – 1 vote as to give it the monopoly of state power until the next round. But even this majority of 50% + 1 is an extreme rarity in the world around us. Most elected majorities have been brought in place through most of the history of the franchise around the "democratic" world by a small or large minority of those who actually cast their vote.

For instance, the BJP's own majority in the 2014 elections was the making of 31% of the votes cast, which makes it about 20-22% of the total electorate or about 14% of the populace—69% or an overwhelming majority did not favour it. In 2019 again, a bigger majority for the BJP has been elected by under 38%—62% did not elect it. But this has been true throughout the past 67 years of the elections since independence.

The Congress under Rajiv Gandhi touched the highest ever score of MPs in 1984, yet without 50% + 1 vote. Indeed, perhaps barring the first two or three elections in South Africa where universal franchise was still very new and the African National Congress won power by a majority of votes (which ultimately gave them a Jacob Zuma), no "free and fair" elections have ever led to governments with a majority of popular vote anywhere.

In the universal role model of democracy, the US, Donald Trump has been elected president by 2.5 million fewer votes than his main competitor, Hillary Clinton. The French Constitution requires the president to be elected by 50% +1 vote, but the rule is not binding on the rest of the government.

Indeed, the rule is not binding on any of the elected representatives, members of parliament or any other body anywhere where such democracy is practiced. How does this then square with democracy's claim to be the rule of the majority, much less the rule of the "people"? And "free and fair" elections come at the end of enormous manipulations and incessant falsehoods of every sort which distort genuinely free and fair electoral choices.

Another problem: "Modernity" creates its self-image by announcing a definitive break from its medieval past which it equates with religion, religiosity and superstition, collectively characterised by it as the Dark Age. The basic claim of medieval Christian or Islamic theology was the monopoly of the single Truth; written in it was universal validity and its inevitable ultimate universal triumph over all "falsehoods".

Much as the rationality of "modernity" denounces the superstitions of the Dark Age, it has unreservedly imbibed the assumption of the single Truth of democracy from theology and therefore the inevitability of its ultimate universal triumph. In the process of achieving it by the use of persuasion or force, it reinforces the theological logic in a new garb. Theology too was not averse to using an immense amount of violence, besides persuasion, to conquer the world.

If democracy asserts the equality of human beings on the principle of individual freedoms, its practice through the single medium of elections eliminates all other anterior egalitarian assertions through history whether in religious or non-religious forms. Paradoxically, if theology had legitimised the divine right of rulers, the underlying principle of monotheism, forcefully articulated in human history several times through Christianity, Islam and Sikhism, is the notion of social equality, even if its descent into practice did not coincide with the theory.

Marxian socialism too asserted the same principle,

though it largely failed in practice. But the aspiration for social equality has kept erupting repeatedly in different civilisations and different times, its failures notwithstanding. By substituting elections as the single expression of the assertion of equality, democracy has put an end to the great diversity of humanity's endeavours to realise its dream.

Yet, what is the alternative to it? Well, that is truly hard to visualise. Ironically, if democracy had challenged the unbridled power and authority of one ruler and created a structure for its percolation down to the last voter, the working of the structure has practically reinvested all power and authority in one individual at the head of government. Elections are mostly contested around individuals, the very antithesis of democracy.

Clearly, evolving structures ensuring decentralisation of power is the fundamental premise of a genuine departure from autocracy, whether medieval or modern. But then evolution is a long historical process and even our present-day democracy took over three or four centuries to arrive at its present state; perhaps before the present century comes to a close, humanity might devise some new modes to overcome its present flaws.

It's Time to Let Rahul Gandhi Go

The Wire, 19.06.2019

At the outset, let me state emphatically that I have grown to admire Rahul Gandhi over the years on several counts: he has emerged as the embodiment of the Nehruvian vision of an inclusive society, with empathy for the underdog, and is keeping alive the overall legacy of the Freedom Movement. And this is just not a pretence; the sincerity of his commitment to it comes through with no artifice attached. All this is in sharp contrast to the currently dominant political leadership in the country.

So, why ask him to go?

I suspect that underlying his insistence on quitting as president of the Congress is his own realisation that the party's dismal failure in the 2019 elections is not a one-off but points to a consistent failure in managing the operative structures for translating his worldview on the ground, what with all his vision for the society, the economy and the politics. Any one failure, even a major one, is entirely entitled to be forgiven in any politician's life. But his failures seem to be endemic.

Over 15 years ago, when Sonia Gandhi grandly spurned the once-in-a-lifetime opportunity to become the prime minister and Manmohan Singh took charge, he offered the young Rahul any ministry of his choice. Rahul declined, partly because of his age and inexperience but largely because he chose to devote his youthful energies to rebuilding the Congress party, as he had announced. He took charge of the youth wing, brought some young new faces on to the public view but the effort ended there.

Very few of them have grown to any visible stature through hard work since then. Ten years of the UPA government, with relative social peace at home and a high approval rating for most of the ten years, Rahul, unencumbered with any responsibility outside the party, had the golden chance to restructure it and sustain an energetic leadership at the local levels upwards to the state levels and to make the results visible. Very little of that happened.

The 2014 election became a watershed moment because the lethargy of the Congress stood in sharp contrast to the upheaval in the Bharatiya Janata Party, where the established leadership of L.K. Advani and M.M. Joshi was being frontally challenged from within by a younger leadership whose ruthless quest for power was unencumbered by any scruples. All the set parameters of political behaviour were being overturned, whether within the party or outside in general.

The failure of the tantrums thrown by Advani confirmed that a new age was emerging in BJP's politics and outside, never mind if it was not pleasant to behold. Every kind of mobilisation, including humongous scale falsehoods, was deployed to save the 'nation'. The Congress party, of which Rahul had become the de facto leader by then, proved totally unequal to this new challenge.

The next five years were a long enough period for the Congress, with the youthful leader at its head, to prepare from the word go to overhaul the party from the ground level upwards and get ready for the next round. The inept governance during that half decade, with one disastrous, ill-conceived measure following upon another, gave him that highly favourable, long stretched out, opportunity to hasten to accomplish what he had set out to do over the previous decade.

Not much happened, except issuing intelligently worded statements. No involvement of masses, no visible line of new leaders, no alternative policy framework, no setting of a challenging agenda that would upset the cart. In other words, it amounted to waiting for the announcement of the next elections which would land power in the hands of the Congress, or at best a coalition led by it, by default.

The Congress did put out an attractive manifesto some two months before the elections began: its timing was evidence of lethargy in the face of a life-and-death contest. Its chief rival, the BJP, begins elections some two or three years ahead and prepares itself both at the micro and the macro level.

Is it then the curtain call for the grand old party? Not really. It still is the largest of opposition parties in parliament and has a very substantial base of political support, some 30%. The BJP's base is short of 40%, higher than the 31% it had in 2014. So Congress is not quite a write off. But what it needs is a complete overhaul from the bottom to the top; and, more important, it needs to invent a new language to reach out to its support base and to enlarge it. It has to break out of the image of the party of the past and to emerge as the party of the future.

Unfortunately, Rahul has failed to inspire that confidence either in the public at large or within his own party, although he put in untiring energy in the two months before the polls. Perhaps he is aware of his more than one-off failure, the appeal to him by the party to go for the overhaul notwithstanding.

Clearly the party knows of the need for a complete break from many of its inherited shortcomings, but does not to know how to go about it. Rahul's (and the Gandhis') departure from the head might spur it to find its way out of its lethargy and the great deal of baggage it carries. Remember—the BJP had only two seats in 1984.

III. Book Reviews

Exploring the Divinity and Magnificence of Love in 'Padmavat'

The Wire, 31.05.2018

Purushottam Agrawal is a new age master of medieval Hindi literature. His work on Kabir some years ago did chart out a road less travelled by numerous scholars; his new work on Malik Muhammad Jayasi's *Padmavat* attests to his durable spirit of intellectual adventure, for here too we encounter a thesis that is mint fresh, carved out from the depths of exploration of medieval Indian literary tropes, symbols and metaphors, the norms of society, and some relevant bits of history.

Agrawal disposes of the widely accepted assumption that since Jayasi is a practicing Sufi, his Padmavat is essentially a work of Sufi symbolism where God is the beloved and man her lover, courting all manner of suffering to win the beloved, with quite a few miraculous events and characters along with an occasional ferocious adversary thrown in. Rani Padmavati, Ratansen and Alauddin Khalji thus get their slots in the love story, but merely as stereotypes.

The story, originating with Jayasi in 1540, then began to metamorphose first into one of an assault on a Rajput king's honour and its defence and later on an assault on the honour of Hindus symbolised in the beautiful rani's body and her supreme sacrifice of life in a jauhar in its defence.

It also got metamorphosed into a defence of the nation in 19th-century Bengal, a theme painstakingly researched by Ramya Srinivasan in her book *The Many Lives of a Rajput Queen*.

Agrawal takes us out of these surrounding woods and tells us emphatically that the story is not of a Sufi premakhyan variety and has even less to do with attacking and defending honour, whether of a woman, a community or even that of a kingdom.

It is, in his view, 'an epic love story' which explores the dignity and magnificence of love. This is not spiritual or divine love which posits a dichotomy between eros and spirituality; Agrawal repeats several times that counterposing spirituality and eros is contrary to the Hindu ideal of their compatibility in a continuum in pursuit of the fourfold ideal of *dharma, artha, kāma, moksha*. He could have added that the dichotomy has really been introduced by Christianity, which counterposes spirituality and even sensuality, not to speak of sexuality, respectively symbolised in man and woman. Padmavat, in pursuit of this compatibility, treats eros and desire as pathways to divinity. Much like the erotic sculptures, paintings and poetry, which are explicit in their depictions without standing at the opposite end of divinity.

This is the central theme of the book and Agrawal lays it out with great élan and very wide-ranging scholarship. Both he and the eminent scholar of Hinduism, Devdutt Pattanaik, who has introduced as well as illustrated the book with charming sketches, have knocked down another widely prevalent dichotomy particularly among historians, one between history and literature, including mythology, as a simple distinction between 'fact' and 'fiction'. The difference between them does not amount to a dichotomy, for each is a reflection of one or another facet of 'reality', which is not merely material but also ideational, even spiritual.

When Chaitanya experiences ecstasy chanting the name of Krishna or when a darvish experiences it in his moment of hāl and seeks fanā' (annihilation of selfhood), that too is a reality for them and I cannot see anyone else's entitlement to question it. Karl Marx's observation in *Capital* III, 'religion is a reflex of the real world' could not have been further off the mark.

Agrawal does not get into the question of the historicity of the story of Padmavati except tangentially. Its historicity is a fact for the likes of Arvind Singh Mewar, who claims to have descended from the beautiful rani, and the so-called Karni Sena who land up in TV studio debates with naked swords in hand to defend their case; there isn't much to debate on it in scholarly pursuits.

Early on in the book—and in the entire text of his book on Kabir—Agrawal places his discussion in the context of what he insists is the evolution of indigenous (or vernacular) or early modernity in India. He locates the agency of this phenomenon in the growth of trade, much like Belgian historian Henri Pirenne had done in the context of Europe in the 1920s and 30s by positing a feudalism-trade dichotomy. There are several problems with this postulate. One, it merely seeks to establish that if Europe had brought in modernity through the agency of trade, we too did the same. Second, and more important, the notion of trade either as a dissolvent of feudalism or a harbinger of 'modernity' was blown to bits in Europe itself within a couple of decades of its formulation. Trade—long-distance trade—has existed in the world from pre-historic times like the Harappan civilisation through the now highly questioned feudal age to modern times: it neither created nor displaced other socio-economic systems.

At any rate, the problematic of modernity itself, for long universally accepted as the gift of Europe to the rest of the world from the 17th-18th centuries onward, is by now an open question. But that is best left to another time. Padmavat stands out as a profound challenge to much received wisdom.

A Portrait of Aurangzeb More Complex than Hindutva's Political Project Will Admit

The Wire, 04.03.2017

"The Aurangzeb of popular memory bears only a faint resemblance to the historical emperor," observes Audrey Truschke near the concluding section of *Aurangzeb: The Man and the Myth*. This indeed is her book's central theme. In the slim volume, Truschke seeks to sift the man from the myth that has grown around him, especially in popular imagination, over the past couple of centuries.

Truschke burst onto the horizon of medieval Indian history studies just a year ago with her major work, *Culture of Encounters: Sanskrit at the Mughal Court*, in which she argues that the Mughal court generally, but especially between 1560 and 1660 (comprising the reigns of Akbar, Jahangir and Shah Jahan), greatly patronised not only the Sanskrit language but Sanskrit culture as part of their vision of governance. She bases her argument on an immense amount of in-depth research. The book is clearly meant for the professional medievalist.

The book under review here, on the other hand, is not only half the size of the first but is equally clearly meant for the lay reader, lighter to read with no footnotes and no complex arguments. As a historian, she is disturbed by the distance between professional knowledge and popular image of the man and the emperor, and intervenes to minimise that distance without being an apologist for either the man or the emperor. "The multifaceted king had a complex relationship with Islam, but even so he is not reducible to his religion. In fact, little is simple about Aurangzeb. Aurangzeb was an emperor devoted to power, his vision of justice, and expansion. He was an administrator with streaks of brilliance and scores of faults. He grew the Mughal Empire to its greatest extent and may also have positioned it to break apart. No single characteristic or action can encapsulate Aurangzeb Alamgir..."

This indeed is the problem with seeking to minimise the distance between a professional estimate and the popular image of a ruler, any ruler. The historian looks at a ruler's reign as constantly evolving in interaction with a whole complex array of opposing pulls and pressures—political, administrative, economic, cultural, religious, factional and so forth. In popular image, the ruler's single characteristic is given and fixed and that characteristic is the unwavering driving force during his reign.

The argument that Aurangzeb's war with his brother and rival Dara Shukoh was not a battle between orthodoxy and liberalism and that the two did not have their support base divided between the orthodox and liberals or the Muslims and the Hindus among the nobles who took sides has long been established in historiography. M. Athar Ali had demonstrated this in his book *Mughal Nobility Under Aurangzeb*, published in 1966. Aurangzeb had the support of 21 Hindu nobles of high ranks, including the legendary Rajputs Jai Singh and Jaswant Singh, and Dara had 24 on his side, none as grand as the two.

That Aurangzeb did not throw out all the Hindus and

Shias from his court and administration on his accession or later is also commonplace among historians. That the number of Hindus in his nobility rose to the highest in Mughal history; that even as he ordered the demolition of a dozen or so temples, including those at Kashi and Mathura and built mosques on their ruins, he was also handing out lands and cash to other temples and maths and to Brahmins is also routinely recounted in history books. Aurangzeb composed a poem in Hindi in which he invokes the blessings of Vishnu, Brahma and Mahesh on his accession (see Manager Pandey, *Mughal Badshahon ki Hindi Kavita*).

Clearly, the emperor Aurangzeb was too multifaceted to be reduced to a single personal/religious identity. Indeed, no ruler ever is. Each ruler is faced with multiple, contradictory choices and is obliged to find an equilibrium among them. Sometimes the equilibrium succeeds; at times it doesn't.

We hardly need to go all the way to the 17th century to appreciate this; much nearer our times, most of us would remember that Prime Minister Rajiv Gandhi, face to face with contradictory pressures from the Muslim clergy on the Shah Bano case and Hindu extremists on the Ram janmabhumi issue opted to placate both simultaneously. He didn't succeed; nor did Aurangzeb. But the attempt on the part of both was to win over two competing sides simultaneously.

Is this too complex an argument for the lay person? Partly yes, for it does not fit into the picture of a single, unchanging characteristic of ruler. But more so, because far from the past shaping the present, it is the present which shapes the past. The political conflicts of the present demand the casting of images of the past. Aurangzeb wasn't perceived as a hardcore religious zealot in his own time by historians, including several Hindu historians such as Bhim Sen and Ishwar Das; this image began to grow in the late 18th century and after, finding a firm footing in the colonial and nationalist historiography of the 20th century.

Today, when the entire political mobilisation of the ruling party is driven by the colonial "divide and rule" strategy and the Rashtriya Swayamsevak Sangh keeps propagating its social vision of the Muslim as the "other", the demonic Aurangzeb comes in handy as the embodiment of all that is evil. History, of course, is everyone's slave; everyone is her master, whether one is trained as an electrician or a dentist or has a PhD in chemical engineering, never mind a lifetime spent by professionals trying to unravel its complexities.

It is here that a learned intervention by a fine scholar such as Truschke to rectify the popular perception of Aurangzeb is likely to meet with resistance. For political exigencies dictate partial memorisation of history. Amnesia about the Marathas' "secular" plunder of everyone they could, a lot of them Hindu rajas in Rajasthan, is almost unmentionable now, although it was part of history books down to the 1950s. But whatever image of Aurangzeb that caters to the political project of a Hindu rashtra will remain in circulation, never mind all the complexities the professional historians unearth. Who says history deals with the past? It is ever present. However, the case for history's truth remains important for those not committed to its RSS version. The book is a valuable aid for arriving at that complex truth.

Babur—The Remarkable Emperor Who Happened to be a Muslim

The Wire, 25.05.2018

Among several other records, Babur could probably be credited with having inspired the largest number of biographies among the long list of emperors of India. *Babur: Timurid Prince and Mughal Emperor* by Stephen Frederic Dale is one more, one which is brief, crisp and easy on the mind's eye. This, by an old hand at the study of "Islamic" empires and societies in West and Central Asia, Iran and India. Giving us a biography of Babur is for him not a new enterprise.

Indeed, his entire quest, combined with an unapologetic age-old style narration of events of his subject, reinforces the impression that while one can look for a good summary of the existing knowledge relating to Babur, one would be hard put to find any new perspectives or new lights. The question with which he begins, "Did Babur always tell the truth?" and the observation that his account is "not absolutely truthful" (pages 5-6), lets you in on his quest, seeking out the absolute truth in history, a la Leopold von Ranke.

His suggestion that Babur "always interpreted events" (page 6) comes forth almost as an allegation. That the Rankean search for history "as it really happened" has repeatedly been revisited by several alternate perspectives at the hands of distinguished historians as well as well-established schools over the 20th century, and that positivist certitudes have yielded space to plurality of inferences seems to Dale not worth engaging with. Voila, that's his choice; so be it.

In the introduction, Dale is largely concerned with the problem of legitimacy of ruling dynasties and their empires. He first dwells on how the Delhi Sultanate lacked the legitimacy that Babur gave his empire, with the argument that frequent change of dynasties during the Sultanate deprived it of legitimacy derived from the longevity of one dynasty, such as the Mughals; besides Babur imparted "a sophisticated Perso-Islamic cultural identity" as a source of legitimacy (pages 10-11).

This is a problematic articulation of legitimacy on several counts: First, conquest of territory was often its own legitimacy in the medieval world. Second, conquest combined with the deployment of Islam by the Sultans gave them 320 years of rule before being displaced by the Mughals.

Thus, if dynasties changed, the state effectively lasted longer than the Mughal empire. Indeed, Dale does concede Islam as a source of Sultans' legitimacy after denying them any. Third, and most important, it is risky to treat legitimacy as a given; it is always varied and constantly varying. Similarly, "cultural florescence" is first denied to the Sultanate by Dale (pages 10-12), then ungrudgingly conceded (pages 15-16).

Dale does, however, bring alive both the day-to-day traumas and triumphs, some victories and many defeats of a remarkable life as well as the core of the man, his persona. Enthroned at the age of 13, he had to fight his kin, friends and foes through most of his teens down to his 30s, at times left with a miserable couple of hundred soldiers, in the end Babur left behind the medieval world's most celebrated empire, also among the most durable. This was also an empire with a different ideological architecture than the one it displaced. If the Sultanate's guiding principle was a combination of repression and Islam, the Mughals combined Islam with paternalism, the latter being the weightier. Starting with Babur, its full blooming had to wait until Akbar's defining reign.

In a biography of Babur published in 2018, it would be hard to escape discussion of the Babri Masjid. Dales does take it head on, though all-too briefly (pages 192-195) under the interesting heading: 'The Babri Masjid and Timurid Ideology'. Like other historians, he does not find much evidence to support the assumption of Babur's construction or commanding Mir Baqi to construct a masjid in Ayodhya at the site of an old Ram Janmabhoomi. The 'Timurid ideology' personified in Babur is summed up by Dale as "Babur's conquest represents Timurid dynastic imperialism of a conqueror who happens to be a Muslim" (page 195). Here Dale does engage in an "interpretation" of evidence instead of merely narrating it and this for me is not an allegation but an appreciation.

Curiously, with his mastery of Persian and Turki, among several languages, Dale chooses to utilise Abu'l Fazl's *Akbar Namah* and *Ain-i Akbari* not in the original Persian but in their English translation by H. Beveridge and H. Blochmann (pages 6-7, 39). No one should be more aware of the shortcomings of often defective translations than Dale.

I found it charming to note that deeply immersed as Dale is in the history of medieval India, he has also imbibed some of our very own Indian English usages: "publically" (page 30); "returned back" (page 38).

'Allahu Akbar' Holds a Mirror to Today's India

The Wire, 25.10.2019

It is perhaps a curious paradox that in today's India, when heaping abuse on medieval India's Muslim rulers—and the Mughals in particular—on TV channels and social media is the sine qua non of fervent patriotism ("Akbar was like Hitler", announced one such profound commentator), some adventurous young scholars are headed in the opposite direction and are digging deep into Mughal history with great empathy and understanding.

Interestingly several of them have not taken to history as a profession; yet theirs is far from the instant history that earns one headlines in the media if it emanates from ministerial or patriotic depths. Retired diplomat T.C.A. Raghvan's masterly study of Bairam Khan and Abdur Rahim Khan-i Khanan in *Attendant Lords* (2017), Natural Sciences trainee Ira Mukhoty's sensitive portrayal of imperial Mughal women in *Daughters of the Sun* (2018), journalist Parvati Sharma's competent biography of *Jahangir, An Intimate Portrait of a Great Mughal* (2018), and now *Allahu Akbar: Understanding the Great Mughal in Today's India* from yet another journalist, Manimugdha Sharma. Perhaps a Freudian response?

Sharma announces at the outset that his is not to be

read as a linear biography of Akbar—though it is that too in spite of him—but how it holds a mirror to today's India, in particular, and elsewhere. This he does in two ways, one by recounting the grandeur of Akbar's vision for his subjects and his empire, and the other, by narrating any event and breaking off into massive distances of space and time and sometimes just about the other day around you, with a touch of affinity with the broken story.

This is a very innovative and charming narrative style that the discipline of history is not used to. Sometimes detours run into pages, at others a quick digression does the trick. Just one illustration: on page 62, Akbar's first major adversary Himu is seated on his elephant at the second decisive battle of Panipat in 1556.

Having noted this, Sharma branches off to various battles fought with the deployment of elephants over the next six pages ranging from Alexander in 326 BC, to Pyrrhus (280 BC), Timur's in 1398 in Delhi going on to Muhammad Shah's confrontation with Nadir Shah in 1739 before returning to Himu and Panipat. None of the details are flippant. Yet elsewhere some delightfully playful asides liven up the narrative: "The new (Afghan) king Islam Shah ... carried out an almost Stalinist purge among the nobility" (p. 33); or with the marriage of the Kachhwaha princess to Akbar, "Acche din (good days) arrived for the Mughals and the Rajputs...".

The heart of this delightfully readable book is, of course, highlighting the vision of the great Mughal who could cut through the various dividing lines within the ruling class and reach out to the subjects. His greatest strength was the ability to think and decide for himself, which always implies a challenge to all modes of received wisdom. The ability to weave one's own way through contentions.

Akbar was in the habit of raising profound philosophical to quotidian questions. If he asked why should Islam, which was the youngest of all religions in his time, have ipso facto primacy over other, much older ones which were imbued with profound philosophic meditation, he also asked why should Persian language script (official court language) have several letters for the same sound instead of having just one, or, why should a man and woman be required to purify themselves with a bath after having sex rather than before? Or why should only sons and not also daughters inherit property from their father? And so on.

But above all Akbar transformed the idiom of governance from one of exercise of unbridled power to one tempered by the notion of paternalism. Akbar was not the inventor of this notion; most civilisations throughout history have nurtured it. But Akbar made it a, or rather the, guiding ideology of his state.

He took it so seriously that he observes that if he had grown mature earlier he would never have married any woman from within his empire for every woman there was like his daughter! Paternalism implied non-discrimination against anyone on any ground. Hence his principle of sulh-i kull, absolute peace for all.

This is the lasting relevance of Akbar's legacy which Sharma has brought out with such charm and which is under threat from the present-day secular democratic state.

He also takes on the various films and TV serials, past and present centred on Akbar, which this reviewer has not been able to bring himself to watch, graphically analyses not only the content but also the intent of these ventures and passes some very critical judgments, including critical appreciation.

Even as the book is empirically very sound, based on in depth research—as indeed all the books mentioned above are—there is the beauty and the holding quality of a grand novel in the writing. Hard to put down and go off to sleep. Its title itself is unusual; forsaking the simpler and common Akbar, it adds Allahu to the name.

Akbar delighted in the double entendre embedded in Allahu Akbar: Allah is as great as Akbar or Akbar is as great as Allah. Once asked by his courtiers to clarify his claim, he smiled and kept silent; on another occasion he actually denied it. Point made: he would have it either way, through silent affirmation and through a strategic denial.

The Enduring Nature of Compassion

The Wire, 24.06.2018

Shah Alam Khan is a professor of orthopaedics at the All India Institute of Medical Sciences, New Delhi. That is, he sets old people's bones and enables them to stand up from their chairs and walk. Not one you would expect would write some soul searching poetry and now an evocative novel that brings you closer to the deepest sorrows brought home to us by human cruelty as well as the most heartfelt joys of being compassionately human.

It is hard to encapsulate the story in a nutshell, for it is far from linear. The major episodes in the Man With the White Beard are the massacres of the most common, helpless Sikhs in Delhi in 1984, the Muslims in Gujarat in 2002 and Christians in Kandhamal in Odisha in 2007—for being Sikh, Muslim and Christian.

The killing was also the handiwork of their fellow citizens, neighbours, friends—also common and normally helpless people galvanised by the guarantee of impunity, for they carried out commissions assigned to them by the guardians of the law at the highest levels. They were also venting out hate and violence embedded deep in them perhaps without them being aware.

But these cruelties are not just abstract violence for Khan; these are minute, devastating images where individual human beings, with names and identities, are flaunting the short-lived power of death over other human beings also with names and identities often known to them. But violence is not able to crush the softer emotions embedded in us; compassion for one.

Khan refrains from putting cruelty or compassion in tight, impermeable boxes of community, religion or class. However, if violence is episodic, compassion is enduring. Khan has the finesse not to invest both cruelty and compassion in the same characters at different points in time; that would be far too mechanistic. For him, humanity is more than an aggregate of individuals. Hence its complexity, evident not in 1984, 2002 and 2007 alone, and not in India alone but through all time and all space.

This slim book encapsulates that complexity magnificently through a microscope. This is not a story of the Truth in contest with falsehood; it is one of truth seeking itself out in a complex milieu. Truth, as Khan describes it, is the nervous pedestrian undecided on whether to cross a busy street or wait for a more opportune moment.

If violence at the ground level haunts the author, he is aware that there is the other end of it too. This is summed up most evocatively in the main character, Kulwanti, entirely rooted in that very ground: 'She still had hope lying somewhere deep in her heart. She believed that this country was too old to be hijacked by hate. It was the land where civilisation had taken birth, and for so many years people had lived in harmony. How and why madness takes over the same people now and then was beyond her comprehension. She thought "We have limited options." Hope was the only choice even if it was a misuse of hope.'

There are also some memorable lines:

"Everybody was loving this new India—the land of the Sensex and dead farmers."

"On this crazy planet, some attain prophethood and some attain madness."

"Religion gave her peace and superstition maintained the integrity of that fragile peace." [This when Khan himself is a practicing atheist. Much like Karl Marx, who characterised religion as the hope of the hopeless and the soul of the soul less, before labelling it the opium of the people]